# A WAY FOR HEALING

## SOME CHRISTIAN FOUNDATIONS

### Robert A. Gillies

## THE HANDSEL PRESS

The Stables, Carberry, EH21 8PY, Scotland

ISBN  1 871828 18 X

British Library Cataloguing in Publication Data:
A catalogue record for this publication is available from the British Library

Typeset in 11pt Garamond at the Stables, Carberry

Printed in Scotland by BPC-AUP Aberdeen Ltd

# CONTENTS

# PREFACE

*A WAY FOR HEALING* is a foundation for Christians who are preparing for involvement in, or who are seeking ways of understanding better, the Christian Ministry of Healing.

*A WAY FOR HEALING* has been developed by Bob Gillies of Saint Andrew's Episcopal Church, St. Andrews, Scotland. It is available for use within any Christian congregation.

# ACKNOWLEDGEMENTS

Andrew Knock and Bob Fyffe, priests in the Scottish Episcopal Church, for material developed by them in their own volumes *The Purpose of Your Church* and *Inside the Acorn* respectively.

Priscilla Robertson and Helen Firth for reading and offering helpful comment on early drafts of this Workbook.

The Congregation and Ministry Team of Saint Andrew's Episcopal Church, St. Andrews.

And to the Drummond Trust, 3 Pitt Terrace, Stirling, whose grant assistance made publication possible.

# INTRODUCTION

No one needs to be an expert before beginning a ministry of healing. Indeed most pastors, priests and ministers exercise a ministry of healing whenever they visit the sick, the housebound, the distressed and the lonely. So too do lay people - though in all probability they are unlikely to acknowledge that what they are doing is an explicit part of the Church's ministry of healing.

This is regrettable, for the ministry of healing ought not to be the preserve of the professional. However there are certain gifts within this ministry that can be put to more confident and so better effect after deliberate preparation in prayer, practice and study.

*A Way For Healing* is a Learning Workbook designed to support a basic and probably 'first' level course on the ministry of healing. Both the Workbook and the course which it outlines seek to develop a deliberate preparation for the ministry of healing in a manner that is accessible both to clergy and laity. The structure and function of a prayer group is described. Seven units for group study and individual reflection - each to last 1½-2 hours - are fully presented. Bible studies follow. The method targeted for this is a shared programme of learning and discovery. If *A Way For Healing* assists congregations in this way then its aim has been achieved.

A great volume of literature of very high quality is being produced on the Ministry of Healing and is supporting this increasing ministry in many Christian congregations and communities throughout the land. Although overlap with this material is inevitable in a volume such as this my deliberate intention has been to restrict the scope of what follows. I have sought to address questions and topics which will of necessity arise as a church community begins to consider, if not establish, a ministry of healing.

I have included in an appendix at the end of this workbook an extremely thoughtful review of *A Way for Healing* written by Professor Richard Bauckham of The University of St. Andrews. Professor Bauckham rightly draws attention to the many areas I could, and perhaps should, have addressed. Much the same has been said by a very good friend Dr. Michele Hampson, a consultant psychiatrist in Nottingham.

After a great deal of reflection I have decided against major additions to the text. Prof. Bauckham and Dr. Hampson have both expressed what will be a need voiced by many readers and users - namely 'give us more'. But the original intention of this workbook was to be an introductory text for those considering the practical development of a ministry of healing, not a fully comprehensive manual.

Seekers for more material will therefore have to look elsewhere to satisfy their yearning! Enough to say that I include Prof. Bauckham's review to help them travel onward in very necessary directions.

But for the moment let me be personal, and to a degree, biographical. I must speak of the life of that congregation out of which *A Way for Healing* has developed.

*A WAY FOR HEALING* has grown out of the life of the congregation and ministry at Saint Andrew's Episcopal Church, St. Andrews. Within the life of this congregation my own awareness of the contemporary need for an active ministry of healing grew. In this sense therefore this Workbook has a firm rooting in an actual Christian community and has grown from lived experience. As it has done so members of the laity and clergy of Saint Andrew's Church required their active ministry to be underpinned by study and shared thought.

This Workbook was originally written to meet this need, but in that it will probably address many of the issues that other congregations will encounter as they consider the development of their own ministry of healing the Workbook will have wider application beyond Saint Andrew's.

But all this notwithstanding it will be appropriate, by way of introduction to the Workbook, for the 'story' of the ministry of healing at St Andrew's Church to be told. At the very least this gives the seven Learning Units that follow a real life context.

> Immediately upon arriving at my new charge I began to pray with people, or to assure them of prayers, when they came to the communion rail to receive the bread and the wine. Those people with whom I did this might be going through some difficulty in their lives. Perhaps an illness; perhaps a tragedy - a bereavement maybe.

Whatever the case, this ministry was appreciated and on one or two occasions led into a short counselling exchange at the communion rail.

Almost two years later a young woman who is chronically ill became suddenly poorly near the end of the main parish service. There was a 'laying on of hands for healing' and because the church kept holy oils the ancient Christian practice of anointing for healing took place.

With this done there seemed little point waiting any longer to develop a more explicit ministry of healing.

Explanations were given in the next few Sunday service sheets and in forthcoming Church magazines. People were invited to ask for prayers for healing. As requests, or inquiries came for healing there would normally be counselling during the week prior to the prayers for healing with the laying on of hands at the subsequent Sunday service. Again this followed the previous practice by taking place at the time of Communion.

Lay and ordained members of the Church's eleven strong Ministry Team give the cup at communion and whoever was next to me doing this at the time of the healing also laid on hands.

The time had also come to develop this ministry within the ministry team. Six members travelled to St. John's Episcopal Church, Alloa where there is an active healing ministry. At Alloa, local church members gave the Saint Andrew's visitors an introduction to their practice and procedure.

Within this, three items were emphasised among others: the need for preparation in prayer, the need for teaching before the extension of the ministry from the rector to other members of the ministry team, and the need for confidentiality.

At Saint Andrew's it was agreed the ministry could continue as it had been, but that a prayer group should be formed to help lay the foundation of the emerging ministry of healing and that I should begin to develop a course to prepare those who might be involved in the healing ministry.

The prayer group that was formed had previously existed in a small but significant way as an intercessory prayer group - firstly for general intercessions, and more latterly to pray for a specific intention.

The time was right for this to evolve into that prayer group which was to become part of the definite foundation of the healing ministry at Saint Andrew's. Accordingly it was moved to a more accessible time and given a more definite structure.

The healing ministry at the communion rail [and elsewhere] continued, as did preparation of the learning course.

The support of a prayer group as a vital part of the development of a ministry of healing should never be underestimated. Indeed it is probably the case the such ministry could not develop without a prayer group to help lay its foundations. In this respect theory is no substitute for the personal experience and testimony of committed Christians. For example, a long-standing member of the congregation wrote the following in a letter to me:

> When I was at school in England we went to the local church called St. Peters in Limpsfield in Surrey... It was a beautiful old church with a large congregation of deeply committed Christians.
>
> One of the things that impressed me and I felt we might be able to copy ... was a Healing Prayer Group. As I remember there was a prayer session each week or fortnight in church, when as many people as possible came to pray for people who were known to be ill or in hospital. They [the ones being prayed for] were often not church people but had had their names put forward by friends.
>
> There was a group of people who were prepared to be contacted at times of crisis day or night to pray for anyone in particular need.
>
> They of course also had regular services when Laying on of Hands was the central part of the service.[1]

So, without being too apologetic about the need for prayer and a prayer group it is my own view that if a church is to engage in a ministry of healing in an active and open way its work will never be far from prayer.

Some might argue that time should now be spent in these pages to justify why this has to be so. However I would contend that there can be no laying on of hands, or anointing without prayer. This applies to other forms of Christian healing too - for example, deliverance, unction, absolution.

However in the counselling situation it may be the case that conversation and listening are more in evidence to the imaginary 'fly on the wall' than is the sort of deliberate prayer that would accompany a laying on of hands for example. But for the Christian counsellor who sees his or her work to be in the context of Christian ministry, prayer will form that foundation upon which the activity of counselling is based even though prayer may not be visible in the counselling.

In the pages which follow a structure for a prayer group is outlined. A timetable is offered and a commentary on the whole process is gently worked through. In later pages passages for Bible teaching are included and notes provided along with a bibliography.

# The Prayer Group

**THE PARTICIPANTS** In all probability the participants will comprise a whole variety of people from a range of backgrounds. Some may be familiar with the Christian ministry of healing - others may not. Some might be familiar with praying aloud in the company of others. Equally some may well be familiar with praying aloud but have yet to discover the stillness of deliberate quiet prayer. Some may be more familiar with the charismatic movement than others.

In addition to everything this range of experience offers, there will be the normal and expected spectrum of personality differences which are present in any group of people!

**LEADERSHIP** Leadership in any Christian group is a thorny and vexed problem. Andrew Knock in *The Purpose of Your Church* deals with this very extensively and much of what he argues in that location will be taken for granted here. Sufficient for me to say that the local pastor, priest or minister should assume direct responsibility for the leadership of this prayer group. Although delegation to others for specific tasks arising from the prayer group may be necessary, the members of the prayer group will look to the leader as a focal figure who will give direction and content to the group as it eases its way towards greater corporate and individual confidence.

**STRUCTURE** Given what has already been said about the variety of people likely to be attending even a small prayer group, the structure of the prayer group is vital if it is to achieve the effect of being that foundation it is intended to be. Several components, present each time the group meets, will help enable this to happen.

**A Clear Aim** The prayer group should have as its aim the laying of a foundation for the church's ministry of healing in that place.

**A Clear Objective** The prayer group should seek to unite the participants in a process and programme of corporate prayer, with teaching and reflection, at a fixed time each week.

**A Clear Method** Each member of the prayer group should have a card in front of them with the timetable of the prayer time. One such is offered below.

**Consistency** Changes in any of these should not be given to the group without discussion in the group. The period of reflection at the end of the time of prayer will offer pointers to enable some 'fine tuning' of the timetable and consideration of the direction of the ministry. This is a very important few minutes.

**Composition** Ideally everyone should know who can come to the group. The experience at Saint Andrew's was that all who eventually might be part of the ministry of healing should support the time of prayer - either by their presence, or by their own prayers if absent. Other church members, from one's own congregation or others, should be welcomed.

From these basic principles the following emerge as features that must be present in the time of prayer:

• It should be committed to God and the service of his kingdom.

• It should contain an introduction and participants should have a short period of reflection towards the end of the time together.

• It should aim to provide variety in both vocal and meditative prayer.

Through all of this the structure should be such as will help unite the group and help lay the foundation for the ministry of healing.

# A TIME OF PRAYER AND PREPARATION

5.30pm      Dedication of the time of prayer to God.
                 Introduction; any notices for information or direction.

5.35pm      Quiet prayers for ourselves:    individually
5.40pm                                         as a community.

5.45pm      Prayers for healing for others: aloud
5.55pm                                         quiet

6.00pm      Prayers of Thanksgiving:       aloud.

6.05pm      Scripture reading and exposition [by the leader]

6.15pm approx.     Prayers for the healing ministry in this church. In this give thanks for any particular blessings received and maybe also include others' names and situations brought to mind as a result of the prayers and bible study above.      aloud, for a few minutes.
                                       quiet, for a few minutes more.

6.25pm      Gentle period of reflection and sharing.

6.30pm      The Grace.

# NOTES FOR THE PRAYER GROUP

The **INTRODUCTION** might well include details of any fine tuning arising as a result of the group's experience gained to date. Equally other important topics such as the need for **confidentiality** might be introduced as the need arises.

The Introduction could well serve as the group's 'notice board', providing it doesn't begin to dominate the remainder of the period of prayer together.

The **BIBLE READING AND EXPOSITION** is important for the teaching that flows into the prayer group's time together. Passages for the group's use are included on later sheets. Some expository notes are also offered, by way of guidance.

The **TIME OF REFLECTION** ought to be a short time of gentle winding down in which group members' insights and discoveries during the time together can be voiced. Equally concerns can be heard and plans made to ensure these are dealt with as soon as possible.

# Unit One

# GOD'S KINGDOM IN HEALING

The immense success of science and technology in the 200 years since the birth of the industrial revolution was made possible by the autonomy of human thought that came of age with the Enlightenment. The impact of this upon the Christian Church has been colossal.

Freedom of thought within the church became possible. No longer did theologians need to look over their shoulders for an *imprimatur* or for approval to a church or doctrinal hierarchy to validate or authorise their work. No longer did church structures have the authority to suspend or stop the independent thought of theologians - much though they might still have wished to try.

Within this scientific, mechanistic and rationalistic world view theologians have sought to reinterpret God's way with the world. It is hardly surprising that many, if not most, have done so in categories whereby God's activity is seen to be taking place within the cause and effect nexus that is part and parcel of the world's process. From such a perspective God's work in the world is entirely immanent, and is (or potentially ought to be) explainable in terms of the scientific world view.

A few other thinkers have argued the case for novelty and newness to be present in God's involvement with the world - defining miracle and the miraculous, signs of God's invasion into our world - as 'disturbing', 'mysterious', 'unfathomable', 'puzzling' and so on. There are also thinkers, not least scientists, who are arguing that the rationalism of the enlightenment is now in eclipse. If so may we now see God's intervention in the world in a different light?

This section will explore such a possibility. When I was preparing this course on the Healing Ministry I was told the following by someone who was recounting his own experience:

> When I was about fifteen I was due to serve at the altar for the Christmas Midnight Mass. The parish priest had given me the church key so that I might arrive early and set the altar ready for the service. It was a cold, still night. I arrived at the church in plenty of time - indeed was first there.
>
> Whilst in the sacristy I heard the church door open, and looking down through the nave saw my own father walk in very much the worse for drink. I went down to speak to him. He was very garrulous, unsteady on his feet and the air smelt of the alcohol on his breath.
>
> People would be arriving soon and my own embarrassment and apprehension could not be measured. As I went back to the sacristy my father was talking aloud to an empty church. Back in the sacristy I stood and prayed to God for help. I can't remember what I said, but it was no more and no less than the desperate prayer of an immature teenager.
>
> The church then went quiet, my father stopped talking. I carried on setting up the altar, noticing as I did so that my father had sat down. As I went back down the church, to the lectern to find the readings I think it was, I went to speak to him again.
>
> He was rational, calm and quite lucid. He showed no sign of being affected by drink and - what is most significant - the air no longer smelt of alcohol.

There could be many interpretations to explain these events. Whilst the father could have been deceiving his son through his behaviour, deception does not account for the cleansing of the air on a still night. Equally the story could have been false and/or the boy deceiving himself. But I now know this boy as a man and it seems less reasonable to conclude deceit when a more plausible explanation is to believe a true story told by a coherent and rational adult about an event in his youth.

This story isn't a 'healing story' in the usual sense. And it neither explains nor proves the truth of miracles. However it does indicate that if God does answer prayer his answer will involve events taking place beyond that framework of cause and effect with which we are more usually familiar.

*In groups of four or five discuss this story and share your feelings and reactions to it. If this is not direct evidence of God at work, consider what alternatives might be plausible.* [Fifteen minutes]

If this story is evidence of God at work, showing a sign of his kingdom close to us, it may disturb and unsettle us. But at another level it need not. In his own ministry Jesus sought to make clear to those with whom he walked and talked, the proximity of God's kingdom.

Because we live frenetic, humdrum, mundane lives in which we variously experience imperfection we may reasonably conclude that God's kingdom is not yet totally available here and now. And yet signs that it is not far away may be found. The above story might be a story of one such.

Equally it follows that if we are only going to experience God's kingdom once we get to heaven there seems little point us praying in the Lord's Prayer, "Thy kingdom come on earth, as it is in heaven". Why pray this prayer if we do not somehow **expect** God's kingdom actually to come on earth?

Some would contend, and I do not count myself among them, that if we say we are praying for God's kingdom to come on earth, we are praying that this world should actually end. God's kingdom would then come with a cataclysmic force and all-consuming power.

If this is the case I can make little sense of what Jesus said and did in relation to his own teaching about the kingdom - particularly in his miracles and in his parable teaching.

For example, in the parable teaching, the kingdom of God is likened to very ordinary scenes "The kingdom of God is like a mustard seed ... like treasure ... like a man sowing a field ..." and so on. And the teaching of Luke in Chapter 17 indicates that the coming of God's kingdom is not 'here' or 'there' but is already 'among us'.

The Kingdom of God is therefore neither 'pie in the sky when you die' nor yet is it exclusively available now.

I would suggest that signs of God's kingdom are around us. They point to how God's future kingdom invades the here and now. Perhaps my story about the boy in the sacristy is one illustration where something of God's kingdom made itself present in his experience. But as I have indicated we must be cautious in saying this.

There is a danger in attempting to look for proofs all around to point up the reality of God's kingdom coming on earth. It is always tempting to do this - instinctively we want to prove to others the reality of what we sincerely believe. Yet the message of Luke 17:20ff is that we should not use such signs as proof texts.

The history of Christianity is replete with examples of those who believed it correct to cite God's action in particular situations where no adequate scientific explanation was currently available. Any such instance of this, including my own story above of the boy in the sacristy should always be taken with care and caution. It is not good theology to seek to plug gaps in knowledge by recourse to speculation upon divine activity. Problems arise later when scientific accounts do become available to explain the events. The previous explanation involving divine cause and effect thereby seems discredited. There is a paradox and a problem here for Christian thought.

And yet, to consider the other side of the argument, are we to deny our experience? If it genuinely is the case that events in our lives point us to situations where we feel God directly intervened ought we not to talk about them? I feel we should. At the very least there is much in the Bible that tells us we should 'test' what God might be giving us, so that we can see whether or not it is from God.

Ian Ramsey, sometime Oxford Professor and Bishop of Durham, outlined a phenomenon which can be described as a 'disclosure situation'. Ramsey refers to ordinary events which can be seen either as ordinary events, or which can be imbued with the qualities of God's activity. Thus with regard to the boy in the sacristy there may indeed be a perfectly rational and scientific explanation of the events that took place that night.

Equally it may be said that here was a situation where God disclosed himself.

It is important not to think of God's self-disclosure happening to 'special' people at special times. If God does show himself and signs of his activity to believers then we can be reasonably confident that as he does so, he need not restrict himself to particular events with these so-called 'special' people.

Maybe then we should begin to look around us with and through the eyes of faith and see whether God is disclosing himself to us through simple and ordinary events. What is needed is that you see the events in different ways.

Ramsey offers an amusing example to illustrate this. He is speaking about different types of bread in French shops.[1]

We have bread like

bread like          and

and bread like

but if we have been superimposing these shapes in telling the story, we shall finish not with bread in a shop, but with a Frenchman:

There is a disclosure: the 'penny drops'.

Seen in different ways the same events might be both ordinary day-to-day events as well as signs of God's kingdom.

*On your own try and identify occasions in your life when you could see God's hand directly at work. If you feel able, be prepared to describe this situation to others with you in the group.*

[Fifteen minutes]

*The situation was* [make some brief notes]:

..................................................................................................
..................................................................................................
..................................................................................................
..................................................................................................
..................................................................................................
..................................................................................................

*At the time of that event did you think God's hand was at work?*

..................................................................................................................

*If not, when did you think it might be?*

..................................................................................................................

*Are there any other aspects of this which you feel it is relevant or necessary to record? Make brief notes:*

..................................................................................................................

..................................................................................................................

..................................................................................................................

..................................................................................................................

..................................................................................................................

*If appropriate discuss your responses with the wider group. How hard was this task? Again, discuss this.*

*Discuss whether it seems right or just artificial to view ordinary events as signs of God's kingdom.*

## Preparation for the next Unit:

A great many of the situations where we have been able to see God, or at least intuit God is at work, involve what might be called 'good things' that have happened to us. But there is a converse side to this. Namely, how do we see God at work in bad situations, or in situations where there is manifest evil?

*In a burst of brainstorming the group should identify as many bad or evil situations as it can. If time permits these should be grouped under at least two headings. One heading should include those situations where human fault is to blame. Another heading should include those situations where human fault took no place in the situation. A third section might include those for which you are undecided.* [Ten minutes]

# Unit Two

# IS THERE A GOOD AND ALL POWERFUL GOD?

There seems to me little doubt that the question as to why a good and all powerful God can allow so much evil in the world is the main problem which people cite as evidence against the existence of God. This is known in summary form as the problem of evil. The second reason which causes people not to believe in God is a bad experience with the clergy or the Church. This last area, regrettable though it is, needs no comment.

For the moment let me unwrap what is meant by the problem of evil. The brainstorm session at the end of last week will have given a brief introduction. To begin we can identify two aspects of the problem of evil: moral evil and natural evil.

## Moral Evil

When an individual, let's call him Joe, kills another person, Mike, we would not necessarily consider that to be an evil act. To make the correct judgment as to whether it was evil or not we would want to find out why Joe behaved the way he did. If for example we discover that Mike was about to shoot Joe's daughter and the only way Joe could prevent the murder was to attack Mike. If in the struggle that resulted say, Joe killed Mike with the gun then we could say it was regrettable but nevertheless understandable given the circumstances.

But if Joe had his own gun and used it on Mike just as he was about to kill Joe's daughter it is likely our attitude and understanding would still be with Joe even though it is possible he may well have been more calculating in his actions.

15

However, consider the possibility that Mike had been Joe's boss at work and Mike had been having an affair with Joe's wife and had been taunting Joe at work about his own sexual successes with Joe's wife. Imagine also that Joe's wife also taunted and teased Joe in the same way. Over a period of several months Joe begins to lose his composure. One day he returns home unexpectedly and finds Mike and his own wife in bed. In a fit of rage he takes the kitchen knife and kills them.

*Can we understand his actions? Can we agree with them? Discuss these questions in three's and be prepared to report back to the wider group.* [Five minutes]

*Would you consider the situation any different if you had been told that Joe had known his wife and Mike were together and that on his way home he had deliberately bought a large cleaver with which to kill them both?*

*Back in your groups of three discuss whether this changes your attitude to Joe's action. Identify any significant difference between the two scenarios. Again be prepared to report back to the wider group.* [Five minutes]

*Let's now imagine another situation involving Mike and Joe. Mike is a security guard delivering, we can assume, a large amount of money to a bank. Joe, intending to steal the money, hits Mike with a fatal blow on the head.*

*Answer the following questions:*

*Did Joe do wrong?* **Yes / No** [delete as appropriate]

*Could Joe have done otherwise?* **Yes / No**

*What might have caused Joe to act in the way he did? Draw up a short list of possible causes:*

...........................................................................................................

...........................................................................................................

...........................................................................................................

*In the wider group discuss whether Joe was exercising his free will when he decided to rob Mike in a way that he might not have been in some of the other examples concerning killing* [Ten minutes]

When someone, or a community of people, deliberately commit some evil this is called **moral evil.** Its cause may be ascribed to human free will.

# Natural Evil

Consider an earthquake, or a volcano suddenly erupting. The cause for either of these cannot be laid at the door of human free will. These are events which are part of natural processes and can cause untold suffering, very often to people least able to withstand the devastation that often results.

But the question arises, if humans are not to blame for these then who is? And people ask, "If God is all loving and all powerful why should he allow such events to happen?"

The following story appeared in *The Times* of April 1st 1993:

> There are some things 18-month-old Dean Griffiths will one day wish he had never been told ... Both his parents are dying from AIDS-related diseases. He may also be HIV positive. When he is tested for the virus, after his second birthday ... the outcome will determine not only how long he has to live, but who will care for him - and how...?
>
> Dean was born healthy, but his parents' health declined as their condition progressed from HIV infection to AIDS... More than 100 children in Britain have died of AIDS and about 450 are infected with HIV.
>
> The Griffithses ... are former drug users ... [they] contracted the infection in 1986 from sharing dirty needles... 'I say my prayers every night', Mrs Griffiths says. 'If the test does come out positive, I could never believe in God again. Why did God allow me to get pregnant when he knew I was HIV positive?

*In the wider group consider whether the Griffiths story is an example of moral or natural evil. Would your opinion be any different if they had contracted HIV/AIDS from a blood transfusion?* [Fifteen minutes]

*In groups of five answer the following:* [max. time fifteen minutes]

*What benefits arise out of suffering?* [Agree a list]

.........................................................................................................

.........................................................................................................

.........................................................................................................

.........................................................................................................

.........................................................................................................

.........................................................................................................

.........................................................................................................

*Also, consider the following statement on your own and honestly record whether or not you agree. Write down any qualification you might have.* [Five minutes]
"For God to want or allow us to suffer in ways that are disproportionate to any benefits gained then I conclude God is not worthy of our worship." **Agree / Disagree**

*Are there any qualifications or notes you might wish to make? If so what are they?*

.........................................................................................................

.........................................................................................................

.........................................................................................................

.........................................................................................................

.........................................................................................................

.........................................................................................................

*Discuss this in the wider group. And then either in the wider group or back in groups of three [as best seems most appropriate at the time] consider whether there is something flawed, or wrong, in God's creation which makes both moral evil and natural evil a reality. If this is discussed in the smaller groups then be prepared to bring the results of the discussion back to the wider group.*

[Twenty minutes]

# Redefining the Power of God

Is the presence of evil in the world an inevitable product [perhaps even by-product] of God's creation? Could it even be the case that God created the best world he could, and that his work in creation was a more loving action than not creating?

Perhaps it is the case that God, like us, has to strive constantly against all sorts of hindrances that are an obstacle to his all-loving will. If he could overcome these hindrances we might wish he should, but he can only work patiently to overcome the ill they bring about by the constant exercise of his love.

These hindrances, which might include human free-will as well as seemingly uncontrollable natural forces, are neither willed nor created by God. They might simply be part of a 'Given' which he encounters. In his struggle to overcome this 'Given', God's omnipotence (his being all-powerful) is limited.

When we think in these terms we are in a tradition which arguably began with the philosopher Locke, passed through the Scots Enlightenment thinker David Hume and is found in the German philosopher Hegel. Jurgen Moltmann in his book *The Power of the Powerless* is a recent expositor of the idea of limitation in God. None however, have been as careful and as sensitive in their approach as has Jan Milic Lochman in his commentary on the creed, *The Faith We Confess*.

Broadly speaking the thrust of these two continental theologians has been to remind us that the ultimate victory of Jesus was won after the apparent defeat of the cross. It was in his weakest hour that Jesus showed to the faithful the power of God at its most triumphant.

This serves to remind us not to look for God's power in great and mighty acts - though it might be there. Rather we should see God's power in the suffering servant bound and incapacitated by nails and a torn side.

It is in this weak, suffering, limited Jesus that we can see God at his most powerful working to bring new life and healing out of the pain of the present world.

Such a view does not necessarily convince doubters but it does at least attempt to reconcile the problem of how a loving God allows so much evil. It may even cause some comfort as the following story from my own experience indicates:

> In my early ministry I regularly visited a house where Bert, the husband, was incapacitated in speech and mobility because of a serious stroke. In due course the wife was diagnosed as having a terminal and very rapid cancer. Whilst I was visiting her in her last hours at the hospital, Bert was brought up from his own ward to see his wife. Her own speech was barely audible. Tears of frustration and despair poured down his cheeks as they held hands.
>
> After he had been taken away she whispered her disbelief in a God who could allow all this. I replied that God, in Jesus, had entered human suffering and knew what it was like from inside.
>
> Whether this convinced or not I will never know but there was a look of new realisation on her face as I spoke.

It is this God of weakness and suffering which faith attests is all-powerful in his ability to overcome the total negation of real and undeniable evil.


# Preparation for the next Unit

*For next week a Bible and a pen/pencil will be needed.*

# Unit Three

# GOD'S HEALING IN THE GOSPELS

Fundamental for any Christian community undertaking an active and explicit ministry of healing is a thorough grounding in the Biblical teaching on healing. For the purposes of this chapter I shall restrict myself specifically to Jesus' teaching in the Gospels.

Jesus came to "further God's purpose of putting things to rights".[1] He came we are told, not to seek his own will "but the will of him who sent me". [John 5:30] This he does not in his own terms but rather in the terms of the Kingdom of God - by Kingdom of God meaning that state of affairs which will pertain once God has visited and redeemed his people and has established a new order in his creation. This is the state, or better - situation, in which God will "wipe every tear from their eyes. There shall be an end to death, and to mourning and crying and pain, for the old order has passed away!" [Revelation 21:4]

In Jesus this situation has already been begun. It is already with us, although it is by no means complete, the "kingdom groans in travail" [Romans 8:22]; it is coming to birth. Signs of it however, were present in Jesus' own ministry for he clearly indicates that the inauguration of God's kingdom is closely bound up with his own life. In response to questions seeking to establish who he was Jesus heals many around him and then sends messengers to John the Baptist to tell him that they have seen and heard "the blind regain their sight, the lame walk, lepers are made clean, the deaf hear, the dead are raised to life, the poor are brought good news ..." [Luke 7:22-23]

The mention of the poor in these verses is not without its significance. Jesus was concerned not only for the poor at a human level; rather he sought to reverse the Judaistic notion that poverty was a sign of God's disfavour. "Blessed are the poor ... the sorrowful ... the gentle ... the hungry and thirsty ... the persecuted the kingdom of heaven is theirs" [Matthew 5:3ff]. And Luke adds the warning "... alas for you who are rich ..." [7:24].

No one will earn the reward of God's kingdom; it will come - indeed has come - as a free and unconditional gift to those who like the prodigal son are prepared to turn to God as their father and accept the loving forgiveness he lovingly offers.

*In groups of three discuss how foreign you feel the notion of God's forgiveness is to people. Whilst it is perhaps the case that people know God's forgiveness is available do people actually feel it as real? If they do not, try and identify why this might be so. Be as personal or as general as you wish.* [Ten minutes]

There is an important passage in Luke 17:20-21 about the kingdom of God: The Pharisees asked Jesus, "When will the kingdom of God come?" He answered, "You cannot tell by observation when the kingdom of God comes. You cannot say, 'Look, here it is,' or 'There it is!' For the kingdom of God is upon you!"

The kingdom of God is not an impenetrable castle amidst the decadence and decay of modern day humanity. Rather it is the case that since God's kingdom is present amongst us it is vulnerable and as open to attack as is anything else that is here in our midst.

*With the person sitting next to you try to relate this teaching to that in the previous session where we viewed Jesus as the suffering servant who conquered through weakness rather than by exercise of supreme power as conventionally understood.*

*Are you able to underline the belief that God's Kingdom comes in Jesus with the same vulnerability of the child in the manger and the dying human on the cross?* [Five minutes]

*Discuss in the wider group problems you may have with this view.*

The kingdom of God has to be something that is looked for. It does not suddenly jump up in front of you. Morris Maddocks quotes the apocryphal *Gospel of Thomas* to support this view: "His disciples said to him: 'When will the Kingdom come?' [Jesus said] 'It will not come by expectation; they will not say: "See here", or "See there". But the Kingdom of the Father is spread upon the earth and men do not see it.' "[2]

> A story is told of the Bishop of St. Andrews who used to instruct candidates on preordination retreats to go into the streets of Perth and identify signs of the kingdom of God. The retreatants were then expected to return and share stories about what they had seen and discovered.

Parables in the Gospel stories offer similes or metaphors in which everyday familiar items may be seen as something to which the Kingdom of God can be likened. If we find it a curious notion that the Kingdom of God can be seen around us we do well to remind ourselves that we frequently pray God's kingdom should come on earth as it [already] is in heaven.

*In quiet imagine yourself as someone who is suffering (perhaps you already are). Describe your symptoms to yourself.*
[Two minutes]

*Now recite to yourself over and over again the words, "Thy kingdom come on earth as it is in heaven".*　[One minute]

*Continue doing this but say instead "Thy kingdom come on me as it is in heaven".*　[One minute]

*In a final reflection ponder what it might mean for your suffering if God's kingdom really did come upon you?*　[Two minutes]

*Now ask yourself what is required for God's Kingdom to come upon you...*　[One minute]

*What do you intend to do about it?*

# How was healing offered and received in the Gospels?

To answer this we shall continue to focus on the Gospel narratives. It will also be necessary to refer to the bible studies at the end of this booklet.

*In groups of three search through the Bible passages on healing at the end of this workbook and classify the passages into the appropriate columns below. Add other passages if you wish, ones that might not have been included in this workbook.*

## How did the healings come about?

| (a) Person's own request | (b) Friend or relative's action. Who? | (c) Jesus' own initiative | (d) Any special features? e.g. secrecy, worship, etc? |
|---|---|---|---|
|  |  |  |  |

*Next in your small groups and then in the wider group identify and discuss the significance of what you have found for the healing ministry in the Church today.*

[Up to one hour for the whole exercise. The leader should apportion time as seems best]

# Unit Four

# HEALING IN THE EARLY CHURCH

The ministry of healing in the early church is fundamentally linked to Jesus' call to those who became his disciples. They were given authority by Jesus [cf Matthew 10:1] to "drive out unclean spirits and to cure every kind of illness and infirmity". They were given the additional instruction [v.8] to "Heal the sick, raise the dead, cleanse lepers, drive out demons".

The relationship between the call to the disciples and the instructions given to them that in what they do they must proclaim the kingdom of God is found both in this passage in Matthew as well as in simpler form in Luke 9:1-2,6:

Calling the Twelve together he gave them power and authority to overcome all demons and to cure diseases, and sent them out to proclaim the kingdom of God and to heal the sick ... So they set out and travelled from village to village, and everywhere they announced the good news and healed the sick.

Jesus' call to the disciples and their sending out is the basis of the subsequent evangelistic work of the church. It is Jesus' command that the kingdom of God should be proclaimed. Even from these brief references it can be seen that part and parcel of this proclamation is the ministry of healing.

Also in these locations Jesus gives instruction to the disciples concerning the way they are to engage their ministry, "Take nothing for the journey ... neither stick nor pack ... bread nor money ... nor second coat ... for those who will not receive you, when you leave their town shake off the dust from your feet as a warning to them". Jesus is here speaking to the disciples in terms of the culture of their day. It is significant that the way by which the ministry of healing should be phrased is in terms of appropriate cultural relevance.

In other words Jesus commands his disciples to engage the proclamation of the Gospel. The way he indicates they should do it is with simplicity and discipline. Those in later generations who feel similarly called will be required to take the same approach.

The twelve came back and reported to Jesus all that happened. The same happened with a further seventy two sent out by him [Luke 10]. Their account is amplified by the joy they obviously felt for what had happened. In turn this is matched by the praise Jesus gave that his work was being carried on by others [vv.17-23]. Morris Maddocks[1] reminds us that this should be no cause for what might turn out to be premature rejoicing but rather to follow the example of Luke 10:23-25 to give thanks by abiding - waiting - on God so that we have the space to see the great things God is doing.

The implication behind what I am saying here is the possibility that the call and command which Jesus gave both to the twelve and to the seventy two is as equally real for their successors and for ourselves. The logic that enables us to understand this can be drawn from many points in the scriptures. One such is in the central section of John's Gospel. In 14:12-14, "In very truth I tell you, whoever has faith in me will do what I am doing; indeed he will do greater things still because I am going to the Father. Anything you ask in my name I will do, so that the Father may be glorified in the Son. If you ask anything in my name I will do it".

Of equal significance are the closing verses of Mark's Gospel "... they went out to proclaim their message far and wide, and the Lord worked with them and confirmed their words by the miracles that followed". In Luke there is a promise that the ggift of the Holy Spirit will come upon his followers arming them with power. The Acts of the Apostles in its own opening verses continues where Luke left off and links this with the mission that is now to develop into the known world.

The account of the descent of this Holy Spirit [Acts 2] is sufficiently well known to need no repetition. But the incredulity on the faces of those who could not comprehend what was happening to the believers is something that can bear some comment.

Peter's address to the incredulous is significant. For he stood up with the eleven [the apostles] to point out that what was happening was genuine religious experience and not the effect of liquor. But further on in his address [2:38-39] they are told that this power given through the gift of the Holy Spirit is both theirs and their childrens "and to all who are far away, to everyone whom the Lord may call".

The same themes reappear very explicitly in 1 Corinthians and Ephesians where different gifts given by the one Holy Spirit can be expected in the body of the believers; including of course, the gift of healing. All these gifts should be used for building up the body of the church so that it might become more really that which it already is - the visible manifestation of the contemporary person of Jesus.

The injunction therefore to those of us who are called by God for his service [ie all Christian believers] is no different than to the disciples of the first generation. We must proclaim God's kingdom and do all that Jesus did and commanded others to do.

The use [ministry] of the gifts given them by God was a visible demonstration of the kingdom of God actually opening up in front of people. That the early church could work in this way was taken as both a sign, and manifestation of the kingdom of God establishing itself among them. The same is no less the case for us.

It is important to recognise also that not everyone is to be given the gift of the Holy Spirit for healing, "There are varieties of gifts ... There are varieties of service ... In each of us the Spirit is seen to be at work for some useful purpose. One through the Spirit, has the gift of wise speech, while another, by the same spirit, can put the deepest knowledge into words ... another, by the one Spirit, gifts of healing, and another miraculous powers ..." And the writer goes on to say, "...all these gifts are the activity of one and the same Spirit, distributing them to each individual at will". [1 Cor.12]

The point is that it is essential for those who have particular gifts to employ them in the service and proclamation of the kingdom and that others with different gifts recognise the necessity of the whole range of gifts given his Church by God.

The early church confronted illness in a way that differs from our own approach. We tend to see illness as a negation of health.

For the early Christians it was something to confront and engage as another way of showing God's loving and healing power. It was a vital part of their missionary and evangelising work.

This theme is taken up in the *Apostolic Constitutions*, an important document probably coming from the late fourth century. Its Chalcedonian orthodoxy is not entirely intact, but in that it draws on earlier material and links it with the post-Roman Empire period its significance is great. The authorship is unknown:

> These gifts were first bestowed upon us the apostles when we were about to preach the gospel to every creature, and afterwards were of necessity afforded to those who had by our means believed; not for the advantage of those who perform them, but for the conviction of the unbelievers, that those whom the word did not persuade, the power of signs might put to shame.[2]

But of all the passages from the New Testament which point to the continuance of the ministry of healing the following from James 5:14-16 serves as a proof text:

> Is one of you ill? Let him send for the elders of the church to pray over him and anoint him with oil in the name of the Lord; the prayer offered in faith will heal the sick man, the Lord will restore him to health, and if he has committed sins they will be forgiven. Therefore confess your sins to one another, and pray for one another, that you may be healed. A good man's prayer is very powerful and effective.

*From your own past try to recall the extent to which teaching on the ministry of healing has been part of your own background. Be quite open and honest as you discuss this in pairs.* [Five minutes]

*Now share this with the wider group* [Five minutes]

It is probably a truism to say that the ministry of healing which was part and parcel of the early church's evangelistic ministry has fallen out of use in the western church. Roger Vaughan[3] summarises this and adds corrective comment. The quotation is lengthy but helpful and informative:

## * The Dispensational view:

Dispensationalism takes the view that there is much variety in the divine economy in the Bible, and that God has dealt differently with people in different eras of Biblical History. The outpouring of healing grace was a particular manifestation of God's love and power in the inaugural period of the Christian Church. It has been described by some as a sort of scaffolding which was needed for the first few centuries of the Church but could then be removed. The problem, of course, with this view is that it is not born out by the facts. God's healing grace can be seen in evidence in every period of the Church's history.

## * The "Saints and Shrines" view:

God's healing grace is poured out in modern times, but is especially manifest at certain places like Walsingham, Lourdes etc. It is also manifest amongst certain very special 'holy' people who are often designated 'saints'. Whilst not wishing to decry the special ministry of certain individuals, or the tremendous blessing that certain holy places have given to people, we must ask ourselves whether God's healing grace is limited in this way? Does emphasis on 'saints' and 'shrines' create a barrier to the healing grace of God being poured out in any congregation at any time?

## * The Sacramental View:

Healing is an outward visible sign of an inward spiritual grace and will be seen most clearly in conjunction with the Sacraments of the Church. Holy Unction is now being given its rightful place as a Sacrament of healing - not a last rite: Confession is being broadened to include healing of memories etc. The Eucharist is the great healing sacrament, and many churches are now including a ministry of healing in the context of Eucharistic Worship. This view is good but it can lead to a "priestly and professional" approach to the ministry of healing.

## * "We are the Body of Christ"

We are all called to ministry by virtue of our Baptism. Every member of the body of Christ has a ministry of reconciliation, prayer, love and healing. This is often combined with the charismatic emphasis that we need the gifts and graces of God to fulfil this ministry. Whilst this view is often seen as a "new" emphasis, it is in fact one which has been part of the church's experience down the ages.

It would be beyond the scope of this short document to identify why all this has been the case but we can ask ourselves certain important questions which arise from that situation:

*Do you feel the church in our country has suffered because the ministry of healing has not been actively present?*

yes / no / other [specify]

.................................................................................................

.................................................................................................

.................................................................................................

.................................................................................................

*Is it your honest view that the church ought to recognise the non-practice of the ministry of healing throughout recent history as a sign of the will of God and should not seek to restore it now?*

yes / no / other [specify]

.................................................................................................

.................................................................................................

.................................................................................................

*Given that churches are increasingly restoring the ministry of healing what most gives you concern about this? Try to be as honest and as open as you can.*

.................................................................................................

.................................................................................................

.................................................................................................

.................................................................................................

.................................................................................................

*Drawing now on what you have just written share as much as you feel able or wish in groups of four.* [Ten minutes]

It is important to recognise in all this that the church today in the restoration of the ministry of healing is seeking to work in faithful continuity with the earliest Christian church. Whilst this may be the dedicated intention it can only be realised through careful preparation and regular self-scrutiny of practice and procedure.

*In groups of three draw up a list of those concerns which you feel ought to be taken into account as your own church begins, or continues to develop, the ministry of healing. The list can contain basic items such as the time of 'healing services' or have more theoretical and perhaps threatening concerns - such as the quality of the teaching material being provided! The main point though, is to be as honest as you can as you work with others to draw up this list.* [Ten minutes]

*Transfer your list to a sheet of flip chart paper. On the page opposite you should write down all that is written on the flip chart paper.*

## Preparation for the next Unit

*In the wider group work through the list of concerns identifying solutions to the easier problems or setting up, for example, 'working parties' to look at more difficult problems before the next meeting.*

*Any 'working parties' set up should report back to the wider group at the start of the next unit.*

# Unit Five

# HEALING IN TODAY'S CHURCH

This unit should begin with any working parties from the previous unit reporting back. Any ideas or proposals they put forward should be agreed or modified and if appropriate taken into account for future planning and or action.

Whatever our personal misgivings about the ministry of healing it is a straightforward fact that an increasing number of churches are restoring it within their regular ministry.

For many years - perhaps too many - the church's ministry to those who were ill has been seen as the preserve of the clergy. Even here the emphasis has often been that of giving comfort and solace through pastoral contact and in some cases anointing prior to death. In the order for The Making of Deacons [The Scottish Book of Common Prayer, 1929] we find it is the deacon's office:

> ... where provision is so made, to search for the sick, poor, and impotent people of the Parish, to intimate their estates, names, and places where they dwell, unto the Priest, that by his exhortation they may be relieved with the alms of the Parishioners, or others.

The *Scottish Book of Common Prayer* also has some very wonderful prayers in liturgical format for 'The Visitation of the Sick' but the very structured format of that order, and the antiquated prose make its regular use of questionable value. Insight into the nature of pastoral care and the ministry of healing in more recent years has rediscovered the power of quiet, silence and more informal approaches for healing that are responsive to differing situations and the needs of those present. I have in seventeen years of ordained ministry, never heard of other clergy using the order for The Visitation of the Sick, except perhaps in a very adjusted and abbreviated way. Nor was it ever referred to in my seminary training.

We have in recent years discovered the positive contribution of lay people in the ministry of healing. It may well be the case that many lay people already were aware of a gift they might have had in this direction and quietly exercised it. But the traditionally hierarchical nature of almost all denominations [in Britain at least] gave little opportunity in most cases for this gift to be openly tested and recognised for what it was.

The following story is the personal testimony of 'Vera' who was encouraged by her vicar in England to 'tell her story of healing'. It took place in 1987:

> About 2 years before Duncan's death he started having nightmares, always the same. He was trapped in the nightmare and could never break out of it. He was clearly reliving his wartime experience. At times he would shout "Don't shoot, we are British". Other things he said made me realise he was going through his Dunkerque evacuation again.
>
> Early one morning he started with his usual nightmare, I did everything I normally did to try and quieten and calm him but nothing worked. Perspiration was pouring off him and he was in a terrible state. So I put my hands on his head and prayed "Please, please God help him to forget Dunkerque and the horrors of war".
>
> Instantly I felt him relax and in a quiet voice he said "I was the last out, bullets were flying all around me". With that he gave a big sigh and flopped back on to his pillow and slept peacefully to morning.

Some notes can be added to this story. In 1963 Duncan had the most serious of several road accidents and by 1985 had progressively become both profoundly deaf and totally blind. He was in a number of different hospitals between 1987 and his death in 1989. His carers reported that during this last two year period he did not suffer any nightmares. Nor did he have any more when at home.

Enquiries with the RAF confirmed that Duncan served with Number 15 Servicing flight in Dunkerque from 12th April 1940. He is believed to have escaped from France on 19th June 1940 returning home via north Africa. The main Dunkerque evacuation was completed on June 5th 1940.

The main concern for those involved in the ministry of healing is to note the wife's prayer. It was specific and aimed at the point of need. This was a prayer offered in sheer desperation, by a carer who was loving someone in sickness and health, till death was to part them. In the Bible study on Peter and John healing the crippled man at the Beautiful Gate in Acts 3: 1-8 we should recognise that they gave the man what he most needed not that for which he asked.

*In groups of three firstly identify whether you feel there are any gaps or problems with the above story about Duncan and be ready to share these with the large group. Secondly identify what problems may arise in the ministry of healing as you try to identify the 'point of need' for which prayers should be asked.*

[Fifteen minutes]

*Discuss your findings in the wider group.*

But there are problems for many when there is no obvious or dramatic healing such as that in Duncan's situation. How are we to respond to this? In situations with which we are familiar it may well be the case that the point of need was identified as far as it could have been and that prayers offered in the most specific way possible still did not effect an apparent healing. Should we say that the person to be healed lacked sufficient faith for the healing to take place? Here is another story:

> Some years ago a couple lost their baby boy in a cot death. With hindsight it is now known that cot deaths can happen if a child is allowed to overheat and if allowed to sleep on their front. In this situation the outside air temperature was approaching minus 20 degrees Centigrade and the baby was very well clothed and lying on his stomach so perhaps the situation could have been different. But the best was done at the time. However a Christian friend of

the family said that if the couple had had more faith and prayed more for the child to live he would have 'come back' to life.

*Discuss in the wider group your feelings about this story.*

[Ten minutes]

In order to discover whether healings should take place in an immediately obvious way, or whether they might take more time, or whether no healing is possible in this world an analogy with medical practice might be informative.

For many people a single visit to a general practitioner is sufficient. The cure [if that is the correct word] may take place because of some action the doctor takes in his or her surgery. Removing gravel from the eye for example, more or less means an instantaneous cure even though some discomfort may persist for a few hours.

It may be that a 'prescription' for medicines is offered, the process of cure beginning with the doctor's diagnosis, his note for the chemist and then the patient follow-through of the prescribed treatment.

The doctor may recognise the possibility of more serious illness and refer the patient to more specialised services, with further treatment taking place in that situation.

It may be that there can be no cure for the particular condition but rather that the person has to take medication to keep the condition in some sort of check and balance to ensure as easy a normal daily life as might be possible in the circumstances. Diabetics are in such a position. So are those suffering from schizophrenia.

Others may suffer permanent pain from which there is no release. Regular attendance may be necessary at a 'pain clinic' to ensure that appropriate treatment is offered to keep the inevitable pain under control as far as may be possible.

For others it may be that their more imminent death can be forecast in a way that is not possible for the majority of people for whom the date of their death is a great uncertainty. Increasingly in medicine resources are being channelled towards the more effective care of the dying.

In all the above areas there are practitioners and support staff who recognise the importance of good patient - medical worker relations and who recognise the significant part that counselling has to play in all of this. In addition almost all of these value the contribution of outsiders [including relatives, clergy, visitors etc] to whatever healing has to take place.

Let us now compare this to the more explicit Christian ministry of healing:

• It may be the case that a single prayer for healing effects complete healing. In Duncan's case his nightmares ceased, even though his blindness, deafness and dementia continued.

• It may be the case that reference or referral to others in the healing ministry is appropriate in situations of complexity and emotional difficulty.

• It may be the case as well that repeated prayers for healing will be necessary in a way that is parallel to the visits that may be necessary to the pain clinic.

• It may be that more exact knowledge of the likelihood of death is the situation and that prayers for healing should be part and parcel of the preparation for healing in the life to come over the ills of the present one.

A story given me by a former nurse helps to bridge the gap between medical care and a pastoral ministry of healing:

As a trainee nurse many years ago I remember working in a cancer ward where a man in his late sixties, who had been diagnosed as having lung cancer many years before, was now in the last stage of his illness. His body was in so much pain even with the powerful drugs that were administered to him, and all of us [the nurses] knew that nothing was going to help this man. One evening when I was on duty I was asked to check him. As I looked at him, at this shell of a man, who to me was a stranger, I thought of all the love and memories that were within this man that I knew nothing about and never would. I wished with all my heart that I could take his pain away. I placed my hands on this poor man's body and asked that he could be taken home. I don't know why I said home and not Heaven, Paradise or to Eternal Life. Home seemed more real to me and more peaceful.

The next day when I returned on duty I was told that the man had died in his sleep that evening. I know some people may say it was just a coincidence, but I know that it was not. I had asked my Heavenly Father to take this man home and He did.

*In groups of three discuss how accurate or adequate you feel the analogy between more strictly 'medical healing' and the Christian ministry of healing is. In particular try to identify whether there are any gaps or other difficulties that cannot be explained by the analogy.* [Ten minutes]

*Report back to the wider group.*

Healing may take many forms however, and we must not be led into thinking that it involves only healing of bodily ailments. For those with psychological or psychiatric disorder or illness the ministry of healing will form part of the network that helps bring wholeness to a fragmented view of the world. There are other situations. One member of the congregation of Saint Andrew's Church, St. Andrews has written the following of her grand-daughter:

> ... I wonder if we always recognise a real-life miracle when it is before our eyes. Nichola starts school tomorrow. When she was born just over five years ago she was desparately ill. At six weeks she was diagnosed as suffering from cystic fibrosis. For almost all her life Church congregations, Christian groups and individuals all over the country have prayed daily for her. No, God hasn't cured her of cystic fibrosis, but what a miracle that over the past five years many crises have been overcome, her family have been able to cope and research has moved forward at a rate that could not possibly have been envisaged five years ago. Yes, Nichola starts school tomorrow, thank God.

For others it is perhaps the memory of the past that is the greatest cause of suffering. In such a situation there is no illness, no disability, no disease. Rather there is the 'pain' caused by a situation that took place at some point in the person's past.

Attending to this type of pain involves a process of emotional healing and rebuilding within the power of the Holy Spirit. In all probability this process will be slow and careful. It will involve the discovery of the past and the owning [the admission] of painful memories and their relationship to the events which caused them. In such situations there will be great anxiety and emotional difficulty so therefore any healing ministry will need to be very carefully applied. Such ministry will also likely involve much by way of follow-up and support.

*In pairs identify and list the difficulties that will present themselves in such a situation as the one that has been described above.*
[Five minutes]

There are other situations of greater complexity. I once heard of an intractable pastoral difficulty. To try to seek a resolution of it a small group of friends met to pray about it. In discussion after prayer the group felt that items which might possibly be part of a divine revelation ought to be discussed with the person concerned in the difficulty. In such a situation the greatest pastoral tact and concern must be expressed when making the approach.

There should be no attempt to claim that what has been given in prayer is, infallibly, divine revelation. Rather, the consideration that it may be should be put to those to whom it might be thought to apply. Nor should it be offered in definitive terms as 'divine revelation' - other descriptive terms should be used as well - e.g. 'a response to prayer', 'maybe a prophecy', 'maybe a vision', or to use the words of Ian Ramsey again, 'a disclosure situation'.

In the case of the situation of which I knew the person felt the prayer group had not heard anything that applied to the situation and therefore those who had been its emissaries were content to let the matter drop. With hindsight it became evident that a large part of the problem was the person's inability to allow the group to minister in the way they felt called to do. What had been revealed to the group might well have been simple human insight. Equally it might have been a testimony to truth revealed to the group through prayer. What is revealed by the spirit must be tested to see if it is from the Lord.

There can be other forms of healing. Here is the story of an actual group who used to meet weekly to pray about their church's healing ministry. The group was an open group so many came and went. This story however, concerns one of the group's core members and is in her own words:

> I had joined the prayer group and had been going for some time but on the 12th March I was proper down as I could never ask any questions. The group prayed for me ... as we were praying I had the most wonderful experience of my life. Our Lord Jesus stood on the altar steps, his right hand on the rail and his left hand at his side and he said as clear as if I would speak to anyone ... 'Edith don't turn round'. so I just sat there and as we sit in a circle he came down from the steps, stood a foot behind one of our members and encircled the group in his arms ... I don't know why he picked me ... but now I can ask questions in the group.

*In the wider group discuss the significance of experiences like this.*
[Five minutes]

Roger Vaughan[1] offers what he calls the 'wholeness diagram' as a circle with four equal divisions each given one of these titles; Relationship with God, Relationship with God's world, Relationship with others, Relationship with self. The circle is a perfect circle and the segments are divided equally. Vaughan's point is that our experience is not likely to match this very precise characterisation. He indicates that whilst Jesus did live up to it, we will be unlikely to and he goes on to ask us to consider where we fall short in our wholeness.

Vaughan's illustration is good, but in detail it is in error for our relationship with God is not an equal with the others in the way his diagram implies. My own modification of it is to see our relationship with God as a circle with a broken circumference. Through this broken circumference pass a whole range of experiences and influences which variously enhance or hinder this relationship. The circle can also be divided into three fluid and variable segments which portray my relationship with others, myself and God's world. The influences of various external influences upon me can be seen surrounding the circumference.

*Look at the circle below, and identify in your own mind which of these influences:*
*(a) enhance your relationship with God.*
*(b) hinder your relationship with God.*

*Add additional items to the circle as you feel appropriate .*

*Next to those that hinder your relationship with God write a 'minus' sign, and to those that enhance it a 'plus' sign.*

*The items that hinder your relationship with God will show themselves in the way they have a negative influence upon you and your relationship with others, yourself or God's world.*

*Now identify how you intend to address them.*

*Do you feel they should be 'healed' to help you along the pathway towards greater wholeness?*

This is a private exercise and should take up to ten minutes to complete.

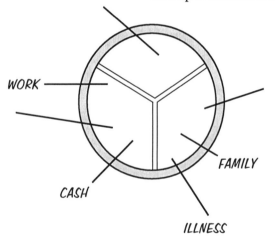

**My relationship with God through his world, in myself and alongside others**

# Unit Six

# AN ACTIVE MINISTRY

It is fundamental that for a ministry of healing to be active it must be soaked in and anchored by prayer. The ministry of healing which takes place in such a context is one that is more definitely attentive to the will of God both for those to be healed and in the ministry of those who actively seek to enable God's will for healing.

There are many ways by which a ministry of healing can be an active ministry. For some the activity will be both a public ministry and a private ministry. For some it will be only private. In what follows I shall expand what is meant by an active ministry.

Intercessory praying may be summarised as praying for others. But let us ask the question, 'If God knows in advance what people need why should we pray for them?' This can be answered at several levels.

If you see someone in the street struggling with a lot of luggage, say, and your own hands are free it is perfectly legitimate for you to offer to help them carry their bags. What you carry doesn't become your property; it still belongs to the person whom you are helping.

What you are doing is seeking to help them get to where they are going that bit more easily and effectively.

Intercessory praying is like this at a very straightforward level. In prayer you mention someone's name [maybe aloud or maybe to yourself in your own mind] and you describe or imagine the burden you either know or believe they are carrying. And then, in your prayer you imaginatively seek to help them with that burden.

*On your own imagine someone you know who is, or has been, in pain. Write their name[s] on a piece of paper. Next, write down a brief description of their pain. [eg "migraine", or "sciatica" or "leg pain because of sports injury" etc]. In this particular exercise try and restrict yourself to 'physical' pain. Now, in your mind, try and imagine how you might seek to help that person carry the burden of that pain.*

*As you do so imagine yourself helping them move towards Jesus - he is in front of you and has his hands stretched forward in healing.*

*When you get to Jesus, imaginatively put the person's burden before him. Take a step back from the person with whom you have been walking and in your mind hold your own hands forward, so that you might share in Jesus' act of healing. Listen to his healing words in your mind as you do this.*

*Now walk back from Jesus, making sure that you leave the burden of pain you helped the person carry behind you as you go.*
[Total time for this exercise, five minutes]
*Repeat the exercise for someone who is mentally, or emotionally hurt. Or you might wish to pray for someone who has been bereaved or in a marriage breakdown, and so on.*
[Five minutes]

*The group leader should take responsibility for directing this exercise. There need be no sharing of what has been prayed about.*

It is important to remember what was said in the previous Unit about the parallel which was made between medical care [where treatment may need to be repeated or continued over a long period] and the ministry of healing. Whilst it is always fundamental that those involved in this ministry should expect a healing openness is required as to the length of time this may take. Indeed it may be the case that many different forms of prayer for the healing will need to take place. Others will be outlined in this unit. We can now develop another:

*The leader should place a low table in the centre of the group with a bowl or plate on it.*

*Each member of the group should write down the name [a Christian name is sufficient] of a person whom you know needs prayer for healing because of some situation, physical or psychological or social or whatever.*

*Write down a brief description of that for which you feel prayers are needed, eg "nervousness", "death of husband", "cancer" etc.*

*Place the piece of paper in the basket on the table and imagine just yourself and Jesus praying for the healing of that person. But recognise that also you are surrounded by others who are also offering people to Jesus for healing. And in this feel yourself to be part of a great crowd of faithful followers of his who seek to share his will for healing.*

*Now go to the table and pick up someone else's piece of paper and repeat the exercise of praying for this other person who may, or may not, be known to you.*

*The leader may use his or her discretion as to whether this exercise should be done in quiet or whether it can be extended to include the vocalising of the prayers on the papers that have been picked up. At the end of the Unit each member should take away with them the paper they picked up to continue praying for them at home.*

[Total time, ten minutes]

Each of these may be private or public exercises in prayer and can be greatly adapted to differing circumstances. The point to note is that active prayer accompanies healing. A hidden reality goes together with an outward showing of God's grace.

A quotation from Morris Maddocks[1] will usefully amplify our thinking behind this practical exercise:

Jesus' healing methods were largely sacramental in nature. He usually healed by word and/or touch. The touch has become 'the laying-on-of-hands', the word is still spoken in Jesus' name ... Mark tells us [6:13] that the disciples used oil when Jesus sent them out on their first tour of duty and although it is never mentioned, it may well be presumed Jesus himself used oil. We might even infer this from the technique used by the Good Samaritan. People also touched Jesus and found healing. The particular instance of this is the woman with the haemorrhage, while in a Marcan summary [6:56] it is noted that people begged Jesus to allow their sick to touch even the fringe of his cloak 'and all those who touched him were cured'. Three times Jesus used saliva, once to make a mud poultice, on the other occasions more to convey his personality than as a direct agent of healing. The faith of the individual, a prayer of thanksgiving, the forgiveness of sins, are further elements that play their part in the healings, but on the whole it is the immediate response of compassion expressed in touch or word that characterises the ministry of Jesus.

Most churches who are active in the public ministry of healing have either particular services for healing or have time set aside often towards the end of the main service of the week for healing. Neither alternative is mutually exclusive.

In either situation it is normally the case that two people would be designated to be available for the healing ministry. Perhaps in a given area of the church people would come for healing ministry. Given this, now work through the following:

*(a) In groups of two, try to identify what might be said by those who come forward for healing.* [Five minutes]

*Report your findings to the wider group.*

*(b) Imagine yourselves to be in church during the ministry of healing and that you are designated to counsel or pray with those who come forward. In different groups of two, identify the appropriate responses to the items raised in (a).* [Ten minutes]

*Report your findings to the wider group.*

*(c) Once more, but in different groups of two, identify the sort of situations presented to you which ought to be 'referred' to the church's clergy or to another situation. How would you go about this?* [Ten minutes]

*(d) In groups of two identify what problems might arise from the need to offer 'an immediate response of compassion' in your own ministry of healing and the need also to avoid hasty actions.* [Five minutes]

*Is it always the case that there should be a laying on of hands or other form of touch?* [Five minutes]

*Discuss this in the wider group.*

Amongst the range of problems that will be presented by those who come forward for the ministry of healing will be the confession of sins committed. The church has always offered Christ's forgiveness to those who repent their sins and intend to lead a new life. This is done at most, if not all, of the main acts of worship in the church in a general way.

The same also takes place at an individual level between priest and penitent. A former Archbishop of Canterbury, Michael Ramsey, once said concerning private confession that 'All may go to confession, none must, but some ought'.[2] In the *Scottish Book of Common Prayer* [1929], there is an order for private confession with absolution. The rubric reads, "Here shall the sick person be moved to make a special confession of his sins, if he feel his conscience troubled with any weighty matter, in this or other like form".

Increasingly it is being realised that there is great value in the private confession of sin to another and for that other to pronounce Christ's forgiveness of sin. At one level this has been formalised in the priest-penitent format. But there may be another way. In the small seminary which Dietrich Bonhoeffer founded in Nazi Germany for those who could not offer support to the Third Reich Bonhoeffer recommended that those in training should use each other for counsel, admonition and in giving the reassurance of Christ's message of forgiveness.

*In groups of two identify what actions you would feel appropriate if someone confessed sins and a priest was not present.*

[Five minutes]

*Report back to the wider group.*

The use of oil, in other words anointing the forehead [usually] of someone who is ill, is an ancient ministry of healing. In the Anglican tradition the oil [olive oil] is blessed by the Bishop on Maundy Thursday and distributed around the diocese. In those churches which keep the oils they are held in a locked aumbry in the church's sanctuary. The anointing of oil is one further aspect of touch in the ministry of healing. It may be performed with the laying on of hands, possibly in more serious situations where a symbolic rite of cleansing is more appropriately required, or as part of the preparation for healing through victory over death. In normal circumstances the Deacon or Priest would administer anointing with oils though not exclusively so.[3]

There may be some who have some anxiety about anointing prior to death [Holy Unction, or The Last Rites as this has been known in the past]. However the beneficial effect anointing might have by way of healing for relatives and maybe nursing staff as they move into bereavement should never be underestimated.

In the next unit we shall consider perhaps the most specialised healing ministry, that of deliverance.

**Bibliography**

Morris Maddocks, *The Christian Healing Ministry*, Chapter Seven.

# Unit Seven

# A MINISTRY OF DELIVERANCE AND HEALING

## Introduction

A short but very comprehensive *Memorandum on Exorcism* for the guidance of the clergy of The Church in Wales quotes from Alec Vidler's *Windsor Sermons*, "You have not really to bother whether the devil is best described as a person, or as a power, or as a supernatural agency - so long as you take him seriously. What you have to do is not to define him but to renounce him. And if you imagine he is leaving you alone at present, and that what I have been saying does not somehow apply to you, remember that will be the greatest feather in his cap. The devil is your opponent, not only your neighbour's."[1]

In a report commissioned by the Archdiocese of York a distinction is drawn between an 'obsession' as something which is caused by "exterior pressures leading to depression or jealousy" and 'possession', "when something has entered in, which is far more serious - and far more rare".[2] In his own experience Morris Maddocks records only one full scale exorcism in his ministry.

## Pastoral Background

It seems to me that one of the problems which surrounds exorcism, or the ministry of deliverance and healing, as it might be more properly called is the high drama that has been reported following some exorcisms, and which have led to disturbing consequences.

In the film *The Exorcist* this drama was exploited to the full in the most bloody and disturbing way imaginable. Some parts of the film were good however. A young Jesuit priest found himself sharing with a priest-archaeologist colleague, and having to address, a struggle between the forces of good [God] and those of evil. The Jesuit was a psychiatrist and rightly examined every possible clinical alternative before reluctantly accepting the inevitability of possession in a little girl whose case was brought to him. As a psychiatrist the Jesuit was well qualified to make his diagnosis. But the film was in error when the lives of the two priests seemed a necessary consequence of the success of the exorcism.

The victory of God over all principalities and powers has been assured through the death and victory over death of his Son. No more sacrifice needs to be made. To use quasi-forensic language demons can be bound and banished, and are incapable of resisting the command to do so.[3]

Even a cursory look at the Biblical material on Jesus' exorcisms indicates the torment that accompanies demonic possession and the possible violence of its removal. This evidence at least should cause one to be wary of moving into the sphere of deliverance ministry without adequate preparation. I have recently re-read the story of an incident in Barnsley, which hit press headlines during my student days, where an exorcism in a church vestry went sadly wrong with deeply distressing consequences.[4]

Mary Pytches offers a healthy warning on the too hasty presumption of demonic presence. She writes, "After the outpouring of the Holy Spirit that we experienced ... in 1981, some of us immediately presumed that any strange manifestation was demonic. At that time we began casting out spirits of fear, anger, lust etc. but many of those we ministered to did not show any marked improvement." And she goes on, "On the other hand beneficial results have been seen in those who have continued with a longer, more gentle ministry that has mostly addressed the hurts of the past. This ministry involves the counsellee in taking responsibility for sin, for renouncing wrong choices or inner vows and for deciding to walk in new ways".[5]

This has to be the correct way to proceed. After all other unnecessary baggage has been cleared away then and only then should the likelihood of demonic possession still be considered if symptoms present themselves. I shall list the symptoms that might indicate demonic possession in a moment, but sufficient to say that like the Jesuit in *The Exorcist* only when every other option has been explored [and treated] should possession be the consideration.

Mary Pytches summarises the way demonic oppression usually manifests itself: "The focus of pain seems to move about the body, the noise is more unnatural, the eyes often turn upwards [though this is not proof], the voice changes and speaks in a threatening or mocking or blaspheming way. Frequently there is a bad odour. The face may reflect a leering visage".[6]

But before I progress any further, we can consider the possession of buildings or places, before returning to people.

One of the Roman Catholic chaplains with whom I shared a higher education chaplaincy was especially gifted at dealing with reports of buildings or rooms being possessed. On investigation, he usually discovered - if it was a room in a hall of residence, say - that there had been some sort of occult activity in it. Maybe a ouija board, maybe tarot cards. Whatever the case the effect upon those who took part was never good. They knew they had dabbled with a power that was greater than they imagined and were very nervous about being in the rooms they had used.

His ministry to them was one of counselling and caution and then the saying of prayers with the sprinkling of holy water in the rooms. There was never any violent manifestation of the sort recorded in the Gospels when possession is associated with persons. The calm authority of a pastor who could draw on the conquering power of Love is all that is needed.

For myself I remember once being urgently called to a house during my curacy at Falkirk, with a report that ornaments were 'flying about'. On arrival there seemed nothing untoward. There were two women in the house; the one who lived there said her husband was at the football match. The other was her friend. They described some bizarre circumstances, which she said her husband would not believe. I too was sceptical and said, taking my leave, that if the manifestations recurred I would come back - but I would require the whole family to be there and would need to return with others from the church. There was no further call from that house. Whilst I have no doubt there was something sinister going on no minister, lay or ordained, should risk personal credibility by being involved in such situations alone.

Another higher education situation involved a senior member of the university staff who was checking through a department vacated as a result of removal elsewhere. The building being checked had once been a large house in which - within very recent memory - there had been a very brutal double murder. Walking through the house on that early evening the member of staff became aware of a 'sinister presence' going through the empty building with him. This went on for some fifteen to twenty minutes until he found nothing [tangible at least] was left behind. He left the building and locked the door and telephoned this to me as soon as he arrived home.

The next day, very quietly I said prayers outside the building for its cleansing and asked God to guard and protect all others who might have to live or work in it.

More recently I contacted this member of staff again so that I might have this story in his own words for this particular Workbook. He said he could not remember the incident. Such is the power of subliminal repression.

But back to people and possession. I have already quoted Mary Pytches with some approval. A volume on the healing ministry by her husband David is one I favour less; it should be treated with caution by those who might find themselves in a healing ministry.

His seemingly automatic assumption that the demonised worldview which pertained in New Testament times should be the basis from which we begin today is one that we must not accept without question. The lesson of *The Exorcist* is an important one; only when every other option has been explored should one consider the possibility of possession.

Even if this criticism of David Pytches seems harsh his 'questionnaire used in healing the oppressed for information-gathering' is, I would argue, very poor practice. In introducing this questionnaire he says, "When an appointment is requested for this ministry, the oppressed person may be given a form such as this to complete and return before the appointment is due, if possible".[7]

The questionnaire is clinically cold, intrusive and if information in it enters the wrong hands serious damage might result. There is no hint of pastoral warmth between counsellor and counsellee. Indeed with such a form to fill in prior to the appointment there is unlikely to be any. Whilst a pastor might wish to make personal notes after an interview these should be in his or her own long-hand and contain only necessary and relevant information. If we take Morris Maddocks at his word that he has only been involved in one full-scale exorcism we can perhaps assume there is no need whatsoever for the sort of questionnaire which Pytches advocates.

In other words, not only does the person considering the possibility of possession in someone need to exhaust every other explanation but they also may need to exclude some very defective Christian teaching on the subject.

But, lest I am drawn into controversy too easily let me restore some objectivity by a consideration of practices within the early Church.

# Exorcism in the Early Church and Modern Rites of Christian Initiation

An important document the *Apostolic Tradition* by Hippolytus, and dated around AD200 contains within it an account of baptismal procedures in the Early Church. It seems, from this document, that the examination of candidates for baptism would be rigorous. Hippolytus tells us that there would be daily exorcism - deemed to be necessary because of the pagan cults and religious practices all around the early Christian communities. Moreover all those who gave protection to these established pagan cults and the deities to whom allegiance was given were all "malignant spirits"[8] who worked through the normal channels of daily life and commerce to subvert the Christian faith. The demons for exorcism in the catechumens [baptismal candidates] would be commanded to depart in the name of Christ by an officer of the church.

Stuart Hall records that the officer may be a senior minister or "junior officers called exorcists, who might have special gifts for managing the mentally sick or deficient, but were probably in most cases merely competent in the minor ritual of exorcising catechumens".[9]

In more recent times the rank, or order of exorcist, was introduced into the training of Roman Catholic priests and a seminarian would be placed into that order during one year of his six to seven year training.

But back in the early Church at the baptism of catechumens the rite of exorcism would once more be performed, with the anointing of oil. It is worth quoting from Hippolytus in full:

> At the hour set for the baptism the bishop shall give thanks over oil and put it into a vessel: this is called the 'oil of thanksgiving'. and he shall take other oil and exorcise it: this is called the 'oil of exorcism'. A deacon shall bring the oil of exorcism, and shall stand at the presbyter's left hand; and another deacon shall take the oil of thanksgiving, and shall stand at the presbyter's right hand. Then the presbyter, taking hold of each of those about to be baptised, shall command him to renounce, saying:
>
> I renounce thee, Satan, and all thy servants and all thy works.
>
> And when he has renounced all these, the presbyter shall anoint him with the oil of exorcism, saying:
>
> Let all spirits depart far from thee.[10]

The baptism then proceeds to full immersion baptism after which there is a further anointing with the 'oil of thanksgiving'.

Whilst at first glance this may seem at long remove from 20th Century thinking the principles of exorcism still remain in Baptismal thinking, albeit in diluted - if not disguised - form. In the *Alternative Services Book* [ASB] of the Church of England, 1980, there is the following. The priest is addressing parents and godparents of infants about to be baptised, or in the case of adult baptism, the candidates themselves:

> Those of you who have come for baptism must affirm your allegiance to Christ and your rejection of all that is evil. Therefore I ask these questions:
>
> Do you turn to Christ? **I turn to Christ.**
>
> Do you repent of your sins? **I repent of my sins.**
>
> Do you renounce evil? **I renounce evil.**
>
> I sign you with the sign of the cross, the sign of Christ. [This is the equivalent of the exorcism in the Hippolytan interrogation.]

Do not be ashamed to confess the faith of Christ crucified.

Fight valiantly under the banner of Christ against, sin, the world and the devil, and continue his faithful soldiers and servants to the end of your lives.

There is a rubric in the ASB which allows for this signing of the cross to take place later in the service, after the baptism itself. A candle is given with the words:

Receive this light. This is to show that you have passed from darkness to light.

Shine as a light in the world to the glory of God the Father.

This later 'signing' in the modern English baptismal service equates with the oil of thanksgiving of Hippolytus. That the two are treated as alternatives in the ASB rather clumsily blurs over the significance of each. Current liturgical thinking in the Scottish Episcopal Church clearly favours developing the theology of the anointing [with oil] after the baptism as a very definite rite of thanksgiving. The anointing with the oil of exorcism may well not figure in the emerging rite.

# Taking the Demonic Seriously

Much material on the alleged ritual abuse of children is to be found both in the national press as well as in more professionally oriented literature. There seems to be significant - though unproven - evidence of the involvement of children in occult religious practices, over and above what might be considered abuse of children in non-ritual circumstances. Whilst some would wish to question the strength and veracity of this evidence, the use of children in occult religious practices is not unknown in history. I am no anthropologist, but I am given to understand that evidence of such practices may be found in other cultures. Perhaps a cautious 'safety first' working axiom for pastors and church workers would be to recognise that Western European culture is no more immune from tendency towards this form of demonic activity than it is from any other destructive human process.

The abuse of children in occult religious practices has been alleged to extend from the most grotesque and obscene forms at one end of the spectrum, where 'covens' (for want of a better word) 'involve' children in their religious ceremonies. The aim would seem to be intimidation, fear and control of the children. Secrecy, and fear of the consequences of revealing what goes on seems to be part and parcel of the abuse. Reports speak of child sacrifice and cultic paedophile prostitution and sadism.

In a much more mild form, and probably much less serious intent we hear of those who might conduct "a series of objective scientific experiments in psychic phenomena".[11]

In addition, there is growing literature concerning youngsters [particularly though not exclusively] who are susceptible to occult promptings and in their rooms, or digs, develop obsessional habits associated with certain forms of occult religious practices. In its extreme forms what they do increasingly takes away the freewill of those [often lonely and vulnerable] who take up the practice. Suicide is an extreme, but not unknown, end result of this.

Now, recall what we said about Hippolytus! In his day the Church recognised the prevalence of demons all around, demons which might seek to undermine and weaken the Christian communities. Move into groups of four and consider the following question in detail:

*Given the increasing secular and Christian literature on the occult ought the church to give greater prominence to a ministry of deliverance and healing than perhaps it has in the recent past?*

[Fifteen minutes]

*In addressing this question you should pay particular reference to all the material that has been outlined in this Unit as well as to your own personal feelings.*

*Exorcism, demonic possession and occult practices are deeply emotive subjects and great care should be taken to listen to what everybody says in your group. It may be that where there is a difference of opinion this should be openly and carefully recognised with the differences being taken away for private and personal reflection and prayer.*

*Share what you have discussed with the wider group*

[Fifteen minutes]

If any member of a 'healing team' begins to feel there may be a possible need for the exercise of a a ministry of deliverance reference should be made to the church leadership - pastor, rector or whomsoever. The lesson of the Barnsley case tells us that caution and prudence are wise watchwords, and I say this even acknowledging what a leading exponent on the ministry of healing, Francis MacNutt, has said to me in correspondence, "In my experience ... deliverance from evil spirits is a fairly common need - not that people are possessed, but that in John Wimber's words, they are 'demonized'."[12] I do not intend to be drawn into a semantic debate as to why demonization need not involve possession, but rest with my advocacy of sustained caution and referral to church leadership as the best policy. Yet it must be conceded that referral to others raises serious problems which must be addressed.

In groups of three discuss:

*Does reference to the Church leadership in situations such as this mean that the confidentiality emphasised in the opening pages of this course has been undermined?* [Fifteen minutes]

*Report back to the wider group.* [Five minutes]

It may be the case that reporting back in either of these situations helps shape agreed policy for the 'healing team'. This section can be concluded with a lengthy case study. The events recounted happened as given here, though I have masked the identity of those involved as well as the location to preserve anonymity. Margaret, the warden of a large college hall of residence, tells her own story. Of necessity the account is lengthy and complicated but careful scrutiny is rewarded.

The account that follows is as objective as I can be and should be read in conjunction with the interpretive comment that follows it as I have tried to separate those observations which have lingered in my memory from the perception of the events as they happened.

"At about 5.50am I was called to a student, Jane, who had been troubled by the behaviour of a fellow student, Karen, during the early hours of the morning. I found Jane shaken but articulate. She explained the Karen had come to her door around 4am calling her name, claiming she had an urgent message from John and that they must go to see him [John was the pastor of a charismatic house church fellowship Karen attended]. Jane was afraid to open the door, claiming she was unwell. Karen remained outside talking and repeating the call, possibly settling down outside Jane's room to wait. Jane said Karen should go and see the assistant warden and Karen duly left.

"When I arrived at Jane's room I found the assistant warden with Jane, but no sign of Karen. I learnt what had been happening and went to look for Karen whilst the assistant warden took Jane to her own quarters.

"I found Karen coming down one of the staircases, her shoulder bag over her shoulder as if she was going out - but without a jacket [it was a cold winter night]. I asked her what was wrong. She said that she had to see the student Jane for whom she had an urgent message from John. She hurried past me, I tried to touch her to catch her attention but she shrank back instantly. She appeared very agitated, a little confused in that she did not seem to recognise me. I asked her how she was; she replied that she was fine and that it was Jane she was worried about. I said I was worried about her, and she glared at me still repeating her message about Jane. I told her I would telephone John for her if she would come and wait with me.

"I left her in the porter's lodge whilst I first of all telephoned the doctor. The on-call doctor directed me to her own doctor to whom I telephoned her distressed state. I told Karen that I had telephoned John and that she would have to wait with me as I did not know him and would not wish to let the wrong man in. We talked intermittently as we waited. She seemed coherent but the relevance of her sentences did not make sense, and she avoided answering direct questions. The doctor came about 6.25am, about twenty minutes after my telephone call to him.

"I expected her to react when she saw that it was not John, but she made no move of recognition or of non-recognition. She followed me into the adjacent office [followed by the doctor] and I left them in there, closing the door behind me as I left them. They were in there barely two minutes when there was a cry, like a scream, followed by others. I rushed back to the office to meet Karen bursting through from the other side attempting to escape and screaming to let her go. She asked to be taken to the Gethsemane Fellowship [Evangelical, Charismatic House Church], of which she was a member.

"She fought with me, my other assistant, Norma, who had just arrived with my husband, Mike as we tried to restrain her, finally forcing her back into the office where I shut the door keeping Norma outside, the doctor and Mike inside. The initial screams and calls for action ["Gethsemane, John, June"] quickly developed into a steady rhythmic screaming time after time. Mike struggled with her finally getting her to the floor away from the windows, and pinned her down. The doctor made out the form for certification and telephoned the hospital, asking for help and an ambulance.

"Karen kept up a steady animal scream for about forty minutes, punctuated by fresh outbreaks of struggling and sudden twists of the head, staring out through her hair at me. These screams alternated with regular screams of 'No, no, no...' They were high pitched, very strong and utterly regular, like a pulse. At their peak the hospital telephoned to say that the ambulance would be about forty five minutes and they were sending two nurses to help.

"During all of this, I either held the door handle, my back against it, facing Karen, only slipping momentarily into the corridor to look for the lights of the ambulance. At one stage the doctor went to his car to get an injection and gave Karen a sedative which began to take effect about 7am. At this time I telephoned a male deputy warden and the bursar to relieve Mike and the doctor - both of whom by this time were very shaken. Karen had now been placed in a chair but the men were holding her wrists and arms. Her screams were less and the rhythmic flow had patches of silence. At no stage did she appear physically different - pale, huge dilated pupils yes, but no breathlessness, no hoarseness, no face colour or limb weakness. In the chair she sat with one leg crossed over the other. At the changeover of men she became violent again lurching out at the bursar and trying to leave her chair. The doctor decided we needed help more quickly and telephoned the police to take her to hospital.

"By now she had lapsed into a different phase - still repeating over and over a series of phrases, but in a more human way. The words were crystal clear, a penetrating thin voice like, 'I want my mummy, I am so sorry, I did not mean it, Please take me back, I am frightened, They are so perfect, I hate myself, I did not mean to do it'. When the doctor asked what she had done, or what she was frightened of, she ignored him, simply turning to another phrase.

"The police came about 8.20am; she reacted when she saw them, struggling between the two men - but she was much more limp, and her feet trailed as the police led her to the van. Once in the police van she collapsed on the seat and was barely conscious on arrival at the hospital."

Margaret adds, again in her own words, a personal reflection on this experience:

Of this experience two things have stuck in my memory. The power of the attack and the sense of engagement with her, as if at times we had locked swords. The most arresting was her sudden stare. There was no emotion, just a look. I found myself consciously returning the look and holding her eyes until she lapsed into screams again. Once she was locked into the screams, I watched her dispassionately, but I did not leave the door: I simply opened it and slipped to the other side, still with my hand on the handle. I had quite rational thoughts as we stood it out, [wishing the ambulance would hurry] wondering if Mike could hold out, tempted to ask the doctor why he was not sedating her, aware of the breakfast staff passing in the corridor. Karen never had the upper hand in an emotional sense. I sensed nothing [no panic, no atmosphere and absolutely no fear]; simply that I would hold the door against her.

Her screams were controlled by a rhythm like a heartbeat, even when the sedation seemed to be taking some hold, her fists kept opening and closing to a similar rhythm. The power of the scream, its high pitched hysteria - short bursts of repeated fire. Her physical strength would have overwhelmed me. But Mike was just able to control her. The force of a bite through a shirt and thick sweater, broke the skin and raised a huge bruise.

Margaret, who belongs to a mainstream Christian church, asks your opinion as to whether this situation involved demonic possession. She tells you that Karen had reported seeing 'faces' - one in particular which she called 'the face of the angel' - the face of this angel being associated with flames. On arrival at college this face changed to the face of a boy, whom she then recognized in the fellowship at Gethsemane. Karen also reported seeing the face of the angel in flames on the pages of a book. Karen also reported that she had seen a vision of a tower and had recognised this near her college. She had also reported hearing messages in monastic style chant. In Karen's room were found various bizarre notes and messages. She also tells you that once Karen had been admitted to hospital the doctors treating her refused admission to all clergy for four days - including the hospital's own chaplain, a pastor of great experience whom the doctors knew and trusted.

Writing further, almost a year after this event, Margaret still recalls the vividness of the event as something totally unlike anything she has experienced before or since. She speaks of her complete sense of inner calm throughout the whole of that dramatic experience. Margaret feels demonic possession might have been present, and that something at college, Karen's own relationships at the fellowship, the 'becoming real of the visions of the face and the tower' formed part of a predisposition in Karen to this.

*In groups of two identify what questions you should ask of Margaret to help you come to a view on whether demonic possession was involved here.* [Fifteen minutes]

*Report back to the wider group.* [Ten minutes]

We can close with a straightforward account of the way two people, untrained and unspecialised, confronted an experience of evil.

Allan, Michael and David were friends at a prestigious Oxford college. They had just begun their final year. Allan had had experience as a medium in a Spiritualist church, and though he did not practice as a medium regularly could manipulate situations through the exercise of psychic powers.

One evening he and Michael had been talking and drinking coffee in Allan's own room. Michael reports that the room began to feel very chilled, almost icy. In fear he went next door to summon David. David joined the two of them and also reports actually feeling the room go cold after he had entered it.

David felt acutely aware of the presence of a power of evil which had to be confronted. He took a bible from Allan's bookcase, turned to and then began reading the Lord's Prayer aloud. They were joined by Peter to whom they told the story. All had the feeling that the evil had been contained. The experience frightened them all. In the morning they went to see the college chaplain whose counsel was "useless". A psychiatrist described the phenomenon as transpersonal hysteria, without attempting to describe its cause.

Speaking about this some twenty years later David says he had never experienced anything like this before nor yet since but recognises it as a genuine encounter with evil - an encounter they 'confronted and contained'. Although familiar with the Scriptures and a notional Christian [from public school days] up to then, this experience was formative in his progression to greater commitment in faith and eventually, to ordination.

Allan's subsequent life has been troubled. Although there has been less recourse to his work as a medium, he has had alcohol trouble and has had a disastrous marriage. Of the others I have no information.

*This now ends the formal part of the Learning Workbook and the course to which it has related. The group which has been following the course may at the end of this session have a general discussion by way of summary and resume of impressions and overall feeling. This might also be linked in with a further discussion to enable and effect forward planning. If all this is felt desirable and time does not permit such a discussion at the end of Unit Seven a further meeting should be arranged.*

**Bibliography**

*A Memorandum on Exorcism, For the guidance of the clergy*, The Church in Wales, 1974.
Morris Maddocks, *The Christian Healing Ministry*, pp.127ff
David Pytches, *Come, Holy Spirit*, pp.196-212
Mary Pytches, *A Healing Fellowship*, pp.127-133
Stuart Hall, *Doctrine and Practice in the Early Church*, pp.18-20
John Richards, *But deliver us from evil*
Hippolytus, *Apostolic Constitution*: 21,22, quoted from *A New Eusebius*, ed. J. Stevenson, SPCK, 1970

# IN CONCLUSION

In this workbook a great deal of material has been summarised and hopefully made accessible both for the lay practitioner as well as for the professional theologian and clergy person.

No precise directions have been given according to which a ministry should evolve and be practised, although it has been appropriate to offer guidelines and give careful warnings.

As the various groups engage the questions that this Learning Workbook has set a *modus operandi* should emerge to give those involved in the ministry of healing in a particular congregation a common understanding.

I have not dealt with questions of leadership of the ministry in particular congregations. Sufficient to say, of my own view, that the pastor in charge of the congregation must have final authority concerning who is, and who ought not to be, involved in the ministry of healing. At times this may be a difficult role to exercise, but no other person in the congregation has the calling for leadership which the pastor has, and no one else is likely to be called to care for and minister to the whole congregation. No one else will have the pastor's overview.

The leadership exercised by this pastor must be open and clear as well as firm and disciplined, but at the same time must be sufficiently free to allow the Holy Spirit room to prompt and provoke into newness of thought and practice.

# BIBLE STUDIES ON HEALING

These are a series of short, directed Bible Studies which can be used at the Prayer Groups. The passage should be carefully read aloud with the leader following the reading with an exposition of the text.

Although this may seem more like a sermon than a Bible Study, in practice members of the group will wish to return to the Bible passage in the prayer time of the prayer groups, and also possibly in the closing reflection, with particular insights gained as a result of listening to the passage and its exposition with brief discussion. Those who prefer to work through a Bible passage with greater discussion will need to adjust the timetable and method appropriately.

In the following passages a very comprehensive range of 'healing situations' are offered to provoke and stimulate thought along with expository notes and comments on the passages.

## John 4:43-54

This miracle is performed at the request of a court official, probably a non-Christian, on behalf of his son. The official trusts Jesus, and perhaps as a consequence Jesus commands the boy's recovery. Later the whole household comes to believe. The miracle is a sign of Jesus' power over sickness and death, a power which he exercises on request, here at the request of a pagan. Jesus demands faith of the official, but not of his son, whom he heals at his father's request. This man's trust affects his whole household. They accept the gift of faith.

The God who healed people through Jesus is the God holding each of us in being. If we can present ourselves and our needs to God, we are more likely to break through to the reality of God's healing powers. That is why Jesus keeps repeating, "Your faith has saved you, go in peace".

In this miracle, the healing comes to the son through the intercession of the father. All should pray for the gift of healing.

There is a tendency to think of healing as a very rare and spectacular kind of gift granted to a few chosen people. While it is true that some have remarkable and rare kinds of healing gift every Christian must be called to be a healer in some way, for the life of Christ is a healing life. Being a good listener, being patient, tolerant, having a sense of humour, being efficient, being interested, being willing to waste time with people, these are just a few of the many ways we can be healers to one another.

[Adapted from Gerard W. Hughes, *Oh God, Why?*, Bible Reading Fellowship, 1993, pp.112-113.

# Luke 11:14-23 [Matthew 12:22]

Whilst many Christians are put off by talk of the devil, or of demons, of exorcisms, or deliverances, there are others who talk of little else. Alec Vidler in one of his *Windsor Sermons* says, "You have not really to bother whether the devil is best described as a person, or as a power, or as a supernatural agency - so long as you take him seriously. What you have to do is not to define him but to renounce him."

Like many others, I hold to the view that rather than seeing, and in a sense affirming therefore, the devil's presence in situations, one should rather seek to incarnate and establish God's presence.

This is a presence which will be seen in an individual's life safeguarded and made coherent because of the wholeness of God's presence rather than the negation and destruction that would result from any demonic tearing apart from inside.

Accordingly when Jesus is accused of being possessed he retorts by an appeal to the coherence and wholeness - the unity - of his ministry with God's purpose.

It is sufficient at the moment to affirm and pronounce God's presence in all things as the most effective means of dislodging any evil handhold and ensuring no demonic foothold is secured.

# John 9:1-41

What is significant in this passage are the number of events and meetings between the man's healing and his eventual coming to praise God in Jesus.
(a) The healing didn't depend on him believing first.
(b) Jesus rejects hereditary notions of sin as the cause of his illness but rather sees in his illness an opportunity for God's power to reveal itself.

# Mark 5:25-33 [Matthew 9:20-22 & Luke 8:42-48]

In contrast to the passage from John 9:1-41 we see that faith is a channel along which God can direct his healing. In this passage we can see that the woman displays her conviction in Jesus as healer even though she attempts to veil her actions with discretion. Instead of confessing her faith publicly she gave testimony of it quietly - or tried to do so. Her action in doing this was sufficient to enable the healing to take place. Jesus recognised this and asked no more of her.

But hard questions arise for us; Why hadn't the healing taken place earlier if her faith was so strong? Why apparently had God made her wait for twelve years for the healing?

# Luke 18:35-43

Here is another passage where faith forms part of the healing process. In this instance the blind man apparently had no knowledge who was near to him. Knowing Jesus to be near he would not stop his prayer of petition for personal healing. The healing was instantaneous and, it seems, dramatic. Whilst the passage can be taken quite literally and at face value it also serves a metaphorical function. Namely that we can sit by the roadside, not seeing who is near. Something in our human condition blinds us from seeing God even though he may be close. However when someone points out to us that Jesus is at hand we might then be led to praise the God whose Word in person he is.

# Luke 14:1-6

This passage contrasts further with the two previous studies. In the one we saw a woman coming, almost furtively for healing. In the second we read of a man demanding Jesus' healing in the most vocal way imaginable. Now we are told that a man sick with dropsy [oedema; watery swelling] was before Jesus when he was at table with a leading pharisee. Jesus, conscious of the likely offence of his actions whilst a guest at another's house, uses this opportunity to challenge the rigorous legalism of the Jewish religious leaders.

The next passage below gives sufficient reasons to explain the purpose of Jesus' questions to the pharisees and lawyers and also explains the silence of their answers. But what is particular in this passage is Jesus taking the man, without him seemingly asking for a healing, and as the Revised English Bible puts it, cured him and sent him away. Perhaps it was that he had sought Jesus out to ask for a healing - but if so it is curious that he would go to a Pharisee's house on the Sabbath to do so. It seems more likely to me that the purpose of this story is to demonstrate the healing of Jesus for those who are prepared to receive it whether or not they have asked for it beforehand.

# Luke 13:10-17

This passage relates very closely with the previous one from Luke 14:1-6. Indeed it is arguably the confusion that is recorded in Luke 13:17 which accounts for the experts' silence in 14:4 & 14:6.

By way of contrast with the healing spoken about in the previous three Bible studies, here is a person who does not seek Jesus, neither calls him, nor yet is taken to him. Rather she is brought forward by him for healing.

As a 'daughter of Abraham' she has an inheritance, something Jesus recognised and pointed to when he recognised she should be released from bondage to that which held her.

Although other Bible studies below will deal with what might be called 'deliverance ministry' we can see in this passage that Jesus drives out that which holds, or possesses the woman with a command and then only secondly, does he lay hands on her for the physical healing.

# Matthew 8:1-16 [Mark 1:30-42 & Luke 4:38-41
## ... and see next bible study below]

A few simple thoughts connect this reading with others to follow in successive Bible Studies. It is worth comparing the reaction of a number of those who were healed to the healing Jesus offers. In this passage are three healing miracles.

(a) The leper asks for healing. Jesus has compassion for him, touches him in the act of healing and then bids him be silent after the healing.

(b) The Centurion, conscious of his position, seeks to justify his inadequacy before Jesus. Jesus in turn makes something of a public example of his witness, seemingly in complete contrast to the silence of the healed leper.

(c) And Peter's mother-in-law. No introduction other than who she was. No obvious request for healing.

All three came to, or were offered, healing - by different routes. But connecting them are the ways each responded in service to God. The leper through his temple offering, the Centurion through his public witness of faith, Peter's mother-in-law through her table service.

# Luke 5:12-16

Part of this narrative overlaps as a parallel with that of Matthew 8: 1-16. But there is in this additional teaching for us. It is not only lepers who are comforted - and healed - by touch. The normal mother finds this a natural ministry to her children, and there must be few men who can envisage comforting the broken-hearted, supporting the weak or helping the afflicted, while they themselves stand with their hands in their pockets! Jesus' actions in touching people and laying hands on them were obviously dictated more by compassion and love than by consciously resorting to a known means of healing. This is the most personal of healing: "For it involves the attention of one person to another. In Christian ministry it involves also the mediation of the love of Christ through the man or woman who is laying on hands to the one who is in need of that attention."[1]

# John 5:1-18 [19ff]

Here we have a situation where Jesus offered healing to someone who we might intuit was not asking for healing. And when the healing is offered the man assumes it is to be in the customary manner of washing - an example of the link between health and cleanliness. Jesus did not even ask for a sign of faith but offered healing immediately. There then follows a discourse about healing on the Sabbath - indeed why should the man be carrying his bed on the Sabbath. It was for doing these things that Jesus began to have to defend himself for healing on the Sabbath.

One feature of this passage is that it is used as a prelude to a long teaching [19-47] about revelation and about his own relationship to the Father. But we must ask why we are told that Jesus healed only one of those who was there. And the man when offered healing assumed Jesus would offer to dip him in the water when its surface was disturbed. And then afterwards the man took Jesus' authority to carry his bed on the Sabbath even though he didn't know who Jesus was.

# Matthew 12:9-16] [Mark 3:1-6 & Luke 6:6-11]

Here is a passage where it seems someone is before Jesus when accusers test him about healing on the Sabbath. There seems a great deal of material concerning the potential controversy of Sabbath healing. If Jesus healed every day, was it only his healings on the Sabbath which caused difficulty with the Temple authorities?

# Matthew 9:2-8 [Mark 2:3-12 & Luke 5:17-26]

Here there is a further indication that it was Jesus' forgiveness of sins in the context of healing which caused him problems with the temple authorities. A man is brought to Jesus by a group of people whose faith is obvious to him. Here there is a message of encouragement to ourselves. When we pray for others we 'bring' them to Jesus for his healing. Whilst our faith does not determine whether or not the healing is effective, we need to be completely committed to the reality that Jesus brings healing. And as we do so it is important to recognise that what we do will bring censure.

# Mark 7:31-37

Here the route which Jesus took is curious, for it is hardly the most direct route. Perhaps Jesus was wanting to avoid publicity in this stage of his travelling. In this sense it contrasts, though does not contradict other healing stories. Perhaps it is rather the case that Jesus was prepared for there to be any and every way towards healing. It is also worth noting here that there is no controversy surrounding the healing. Rather a sense of wonder. The use of spittle and touch is typical of the period.

# Mark 8:22-26

Here Jesus uses both spittle as ointment as well as the laying on of hands to effect the healing. The healing is followed by Jesus' command to the man for quiet after the healing has taken place.

# Luke 17:11-19

This story has great allegorical significance along with moral teaching; namely that those who ask for healing should also respond with praise and thanksgiving to God for what he has done.

# Luke 22:49-51

This is one of the few recorded healings to take place at the end of Jesus' ministry. In the Gospels most are recorded in the earlier part of his work, almost all being absent from the passion narratives. This is an exception. Is this the only healing miracle where Jesus responds to an act of violence? Luke is the only one of the four Gospels to include the healing - the others recording only the attack. However if one reads beyond the actual attack in each of the Gospels it becomes clear that Jesus uses this occasion to rebuke those who need to use might and power to attack a man who is without arms himself. By taking his stance in this way he asserts his own authority over the principalities and powers of political force not only by what he says, but for the injured soldier by a simple touch.

# Matthew 10:1-8ff and Luke 9:1-6

These are parallel accounts of the commission to the twelve to go out in Jesus name. It is useful to reflect on the extent to which we should attend to the detail given as a model for a healing ministry. Reference may also be made to the commissioning of the seventy two in Luke 10.

# Luke 9:10 and Luke 10:17-24

Not only do those who are commissioned report back but Jesus encourages them to rejoice for what has been done through them in his name and also rejoices himself.

# Matthew 15:29-39

This is a double narrative. Firstly an account of numerous healings and then what might be called a feeding miracle. A wide range of interpretations is possible.

# John 20:24-29 and 1 Peter 2:24c

At first sight the story of Thomas doubting may not seem a healing story in the conventionally understood sense. Thomas is the archetypal sceptic who demands proof before he can accept Christian commitment.

And yet it seems he remained with the [very enthusiastic] group of early Christian believers until that day when the risen Lord appeared to him. Jesus responded to Thomas' preconditions for belief by offering him his hands and side so that Thomas might test their reality for himself. We are not told whether he did so or not, but it seems that on being offered the opportunity Thomas responded with the affirmation of faith, 'My Lord and My God'.

Is a movement into faith from scepticism a healing? Again not in the conventional sense, but by looking at the brief sentence from 1 Peter we can see how Thomas was 'healed' by the wounds of Jesus.

# Acts 3:1-10

v.1 Peter and John were devout believers who attended the Temple to pray. It was approximately three o'clock in the afternoon, time for the second sacrifice of the day and public prayer.

v.2 Crossing the spacious courtyard of the Gentiles they came to the door known as the Beautiful Gate, the access to the courtyard for the women. Here lay the lame man. For the people of Israel, sickness was thought to be punishment for sin. Because this lame man was crippled from birth, he must be the son of sinful parents or else have sinned within the womb, said the Rabbis. Therefore he was excluded from the Temple. The lame man's condition obliged him to depend on others to be able to exist - on those who brought him every day to beg and on those who gave him alms.

vv.3-6 Peter and John had no money to give him but they had the 'name of Jesus'. In Hebrew thought the name of a person represented his or her qualities. Invoking the name of Jesus meant bringing forth his power. It was their relationship with Jesus that gave them the confidence to act for the benefit of someone in need.

v.7 The moment his legs were healed the man could move for himself. he received much more than physical healing - the entrance to the Temple was open to him and he was able to worship God - he received his human dignity in the community and he received his independence - he could participate in his society. Peter and John acted as instruments for the will of God to heal the man.

vv.11f. Peter used the incident to explain faith in Christ to those who were not believers.

In the Bible healing and salvation are synonymous. Healing cannot happen without involving the whole of a person - physical, mental and spiritual - including reconciliation with God, with himself, and with the community. For this lame man healing also involved being able to go to worship in the temple

# Acts 3:11-16

It is interesting to observe how the man from the narrative of Acts 3:1-10 'clings' to Peter and John. It is almost as though once they leave him he fears his condition will return. Perhaps innevitably the incident draws a crowd - and Peter, anxious to stop any further attraction towards himself directs the people towards the power of God. He begins by identifying the Jewish lineage - something they all share. He invokes part of the passion of Jesus by way of making a charge against the same people who were responsible for the death of Jesus. But he goes on to affirm the resurrection life of Jesus. Shared by others and lived in the name of Jesus, this life can awaken faith and give strength - bringing healing where previously sickness ruled.

No special practices are required for a ministry of healing [understood in its widest sense] to take place. Indeed when such a 'ministry' is undertaken [often not regarded as such], many church members would share Peter's reaction, 'Why are your staring at us as though we had made this man walk through our own power or holiness?' And yet others would affirm that certain people, and places, can be channels through which God's healing can most visibly flow ...

# Acts 5:14-16

The faith and increase of the believing community is clearly linked to the ministry of healing and the person of Peter as a healer is given prominence. We might wish to question whether this is appropriate, and ask how we might react if we are treated in the same way as Peter.

# Acts 16:11-40

Philippi was a Roman colony, with Roman social and political organisation. It lay on the main road across northern Greece and was an important centre of trade and administration. The author uses a political vocabulary which translates the Roman terms naturally into Greek.

Lydia is the first character in this passage. Having been given the gift of faith - received salvation - she extends the gift of hospitality.

Then the slave-girl. Was she possessed or mentally sick? Either way her healing would affect her owner's income.

The jailer came to faith and offered to Paul and Silas not only the gift of hospitality but also a cleansing of their wounds. And as if in a parallel Paul and Silas we can assume, baptised him and his whole household. [Compare this with Lydia above where baptisms accompany hospitality with accommodation and food.]

In the morning Paul and Silas demanded their rights as Roman citizens and exacted an apology.

Here the healing of the tormented slave-girl is a clear healing. But Lydia and the jailer coming to faith are also healings in that they involve coming to faith in the Gospel of Jesus. Equally, Paul and Silas could not leave the jail without pointing out the injustice they had suffered at the hands of the city authorities. Could it be that where there is injustice it must be identified as a precondition for healing...?

What sort of church does this passage portray? One person has spoken of a Mississippi Paddle Steamer as an image of the church. A slow, bulky boat chugging its way along a murky, dirty river. It's full of all sorts of people - passengers, workers, visitors, hangers-on etc. They variously get on and off and contribute to its teeming life - supporting, disagreeing, brawling and as a church, finding ways of being and becoming Christian.

# Acts 28:1-6

The Maltese locals would have spoken a Punic or Phoenecian dialect which would be 'Barbarian' to a Greek. There may have been poisonous snakes in Malta then, though there are none now. Equally Luke may have thought a snake such as the Coronella Austriaca to be poisonous. An exactly similar incident is recorded as having happened to Bishop Philip Strong of Papua New Guinea in recent years.[2] It is the case that non-poisonous snakes may bite in exactly the same way as non-poisonous lizards. Viewed in such a light the account becomes rationally plausible.

# Acts 28:7-10

The narrative - like so many of the healing narratives - is brief in its presentation of facts and conspicuously silent on interpretation and rationale.

# Philemon

vv.1-4 Paul writes to Philemon with words of encouragement, almost words of tactical or diplomatic seduction.

v.5 Although Paul feels he can dictate terms to Philemon, in v9 he appeals to Philemon's rational sense.

v.10 Paul pleads the cause of Onesimus [the name means 'Useful'], apparently Philemon's former slave. Onesimus is now a Christian convert [v.16] and Paul wishes Philemon to have Onesimus back as a brother and a Christian - no longer as a slave.

Philemon it seems, assumes ownership of slaves as normal. Paul and Philemon will have a strained relationship for having become the father in Christ of Philemon's former slave. Philemon we presume will be angry with Onesimus for having left him.

v.19 Despite his tactical introduction Paul is still prepared to remind Philemon of his own authority.

We are not told how the story ends - it seems that Paul, impotent to intervene personally because of his imprisonment, can only set up the conditions for a healing to take place and trust in God for the rest.

[These studies from Acts 3:1-10; Acts 16:11-40 & Philemon were adapted from the *World Day of Prayer* 1993 Bible study sheets.]

# Acts 9:32-35

This is one of the few accounts of healing accorded to the apostles and given in detail. Peter's recorded immediate action of healing would imply this was a frequent part of his ministry 'in the Name of Jesus Christ'. The healing serves the growing missionary and evangelistic work of the early church.

# Acts 9:36-42

There is a geographical link at least with the narrative of Acts 9: 32-35, namely the proximity of Joppa and Lydda. The authority of Peter is obviously recognised for he is the one who is called, and on arrival takes obvious charge of the situation. Dorcas is well respected for her good works and her return to life would have caused great relief to the Joppa Christians. Once again the healing is used in the missionary and evangelistic work of the church. From a twentieth century perspective we must question the credibility of resuscitating corpses. David Pytches in *Come, Holy Spirit* sees the gradual overcoming of death by the increase of corpse resuscitation as evidence of the advancing kingdom of God. However the examples he gives are less than convincing and we must question whether the return to a life of a person this side of the grave is evidence of a victory over death. Rather I would argue that victory over death beyond the grave ought to be sufficient testimony even if such cannot constitute either proof or evidence.

# Mark 5:21-24, 35-43
## [Matthew 9:18-19, 23-26; Luke 8:40-42, 49-56]

This account is the raising of Jairus' daughter. It 'sandwiches' the narrative of the healing of the woman with the haemorrhage there being parallel themes between the two - the woman with the twelve year haemorrhage receiving healing and health, likewise the twelve year old girl. Morna Hooker writes, 'The story raises obvious problems: was the child really dead? Matthew and Luke interpreted the narrative in this way, and it seems unlikely that Mark intended anything else. Whether or not the story developed from a narrative about a child in a coma, as many have suggested, it is now impossible to make any judgment about the origin of the story on the basis of Mark's account, and speculations about this cannot help us to understand his interpretation of the story'.[3]

The Lucan and Matthean accounts are quite clear the child was dead, unlike the implicit ambiguity of Mark speaking of the girl at 'death's door'.

At times of serious questioning and lack of Christian faith [late Middle Ages and 17th/18th Century and in millenarian attitudes towards belief] when believers consider the possibility of the resuscitation of corpses credibility is sought for them by linkage with a story about the ministry of Jesus. Serious questions must arise in our own minds though, if we consider such ministry is repeatable or even appropriate today.

# John 11:1-44; cf John 12:1-2, 17-19

In John's Gospel there is no record of the raising [one could say the revivification] of Jairus' daughter. Correspondingly in the three synoptic Gospels there is no record of the raising of Lazarus.

The passage is long and is likely of later authorship than the Jairus accounts. There is a great deal of resurrection teaching in it and, whether or not the narrative records an actual historical event, we can be sure that the author of John's Gospel uses it as a sign of the resurrection that is to come.

In all the revivification miracles questions are raised about the possible over-emphasis of physical healing! There are the 'uncomfortable words' of Mark 9 when Jesus is recorded as having said that it is better to be maimed or crippled or to have lost one eye than be physiologically intact but ignorant of the kingdom of God. New life, whether that be rededication to Christ in this life or healing in another life perhaps, is to be preferred to restoring the physical body.

# Luke 7:11-23

The raising of the widow's son at Nain is a passage peculiar to Luke. After healing a man at the point of death, Jesus raises one about to be buried. This is not unlike the raising of Lazarus in John and is in the great prophetic tradition of Elijah and Elishah. Equally parts of the text are reminiscent of the raising of Dorcas in Acts 9 [see p.74 above]. Mention of the compassion of Jesus is significant in this passage; it is not always referred to when he heals.

We can note also the question which John addressed to Jesus after this healing. Jesus' response it seems was further healings. The two disciples referred to here may represent the need for two witnesses required by the Torah for establishing truth [cf. Deuteronomy 19:15]. They are told to return to John and give him the testimony of Jesus' actions and the blessings of faith. Is verse 22 an echo of Isaiah 35:5-6?

# Mark 1:21-28 [Luke 4:31-37]

Belief in demons was widespread in Judaism at the time of Jesus, having been developed over several centuries. It helped explain both evil and the sufferings to which the people were variously exposed. It is likely the case that possession would be invoked as a reason for mental illness, which though not commonly the case today is certainly not ruled out.

This is the first 'healing', better described as a 'deliverance' or as an exorcism, recorded by both Mark and Luke, though in Luke there is a gradual build up to it so that one is hardly surprised to find it. For example, it is recorded not long after the temptation of Jesus by Satan in the desert. The violence of the possession and its removal serve as a salutary caution to any who might follow such ministry today.

Even though exorcisms would not be uncommon either before or after Jesus, the crowd recognised in his authority a 'new teaching'.

# Mark 7:24-30 [Matthew 15:21-28]

This is a complex passage and deserves careful scrutiny. This is the only occasion in the gospels when Jesus entered Gentile territory, albeit the mixed population area of Tyre. There is probably a link between this passage and Mark 7:1-23 where Jesus challenged the distinction in Levitical law between that deemed clean and that deemed unclean. If cleanliness of this sort is a human convention then the distinction between Jew and Gentile also falls down. The importance of this for the passage here is very real for it is one of a number which point to the inevitable extension of Jesus' ministry to the Gentiles.

And yet despite this inevitability, Jesus seems reluctant to help the woman. She is asking for a cure outside Jesus' own call to Israel to repent and believe the gospel. The woman would be a Phoenician from Syria. She asks Jesus to drive the demon out of her daughter. His seemingly haughty reply is that the house of Israel must first of all be served by him - and that food offered to the Jews by him, should not be thrown to Gentile 'dogs'[an unflattering Jewish term for Gentiles].

But the woman, unbowed, responds by calling him Lord, or Sir [*Kyrie*], and accepting his terms of reference for the priority of mission to Israel points out that even whilst the children are feeding from the table, the dogs can feed around the scraps that have fallen from it.

By implication she accepts his appellation as a dog, but points out to him that despite the need he has to feed the children of Israel first, this should not exclude him from offering scraps to such as her. Her faith that he both can and will do this is rewarded.

The exorcism performed by Jesus at a distance is not unlike other healings of Gentiles in Matthew 8:5-13 [Luke 7:1-10].

# Mark 9:14-27 [Matthew 17:14-18]

Here Jesus once more responds to a petition from a parent to remove evil spirits from a possessed child. Jesus' mastery over the demon is contrasted with the disciples own inability to cope with the situation, even though they had previously been given authority to do so [6:7]. In this sense the story also serves to document the way Jesus trained, or formed, his followers for discipleship.

At the private debriefing with the disciples later they ask why they could not drive the demon out. Jesus then expands on the previous conversation with the boy's father about belief [faith] by adding to it the need for prayer to exorcise.

The sight of the boy 'like a corpse' has similarities with the raising of Jairus' daughter in 5:39ff. Textually the passage has a number of interesting features: there are two accounts of the symptoms, and two references to the crowd which seem more like editorial redaction than development of a theme.

# Mark 9:38-42 [Luke 9:49f]

Central in this passage is the theme of discipleship. We might ask whether certain of the disciple were trying to secure their own guardianship of certain aspects of ministry. If so, Jesus rebukes them and vindicates this anonymous exorcist. The text itself makes quite clear that ministry exercised in the name of Jesus validates that ministry. Were the disciples becoming too cliquish?

This passage should be compared with Numbers 11:26-30.

Perhaps also the influence of linguistic redaction within the early church on this text is evident in the phrase 'following us' rather than 'following you'.

The saying in verse 40 is given in reverse in Matthew 12:30 and its parallel, Luke 11:23, and see also 9:50. The following from Cicero, *Oratio pro Ligario*, is significant as well, 'We have often heard you say that, while we considered all who were not with us as our enemies, you considered all who were not against you as your friends'.

# Matthew 9:32-34

The sense of astonishment Jesus caused in the performance of exorcisms is recorded here, as elsewhere.

# Luke 11:14-23 and 24-26
## [Matthew 12:22 and 23-30]

The Matthean narrative is brief in the extreme. Luke also recounts the exorcism with brevity. But both develop the conversation that follows it at length; His power is greater than that of Satan. He can call on the unity of the Godhead as the source of his power. The metaphor of armour for protection against Satan is brought in - a motif which appears with great force in Paul's letters.

The wandering state of spirits is vividly described. When there is a driving out of spirits all else in the possessed person must be cleansed so that there can be no foothold for the spirits to relocate themselves.

# Acts 8:4-13

Here it is Philip who heals and drives out demons. We should read this passage in the knowledge that as the early church grew it saw the need to exorcise the evil that was all around it in pagan society from it so that the purity and integrity of the Christian faith could be seen to remain intact.

# Mark 9:42-48

This is an interesting passage which gives much food for thought. The millstone - most likely to have been a large one hauled around its centrepole by a donkey would have been extremely heavy. Even if not this but one of the small millstones more commonly used by woman for hand grinding the weight would have made swimming impossible for anyone who was to suffer execution through drowning - a form of punishment used by the Romans. It seems from the text that a worse fate is due those who make Christians deny their faith.

The use of mutilation by amputation was an alternative to the death sentence. Gehenna was a valley near Jerusalem where human sacrifices were once offered to the god Moloch. After Josiah's reform it became a city rubbish tip [2 Kings 23:10] where fires burned continually. It should be noted that nothing is said here about eternal punishment - it is the fire that destroys the filth of the rubbish pit [the fire of purification] which is unquenchable, not the torment of punishment.

How does the passage relate to healing? It challenges contemporary idols such as bodily fitness and physical beauty. It challenges those of us who would seek physical recovery as the proof of God's healing. It may be that our healing in the form of personal wholeness and holiness comes through some loss of mobility, or physical incapacity; possibly even through the loss of physical life. The attainment of personal wholeness in and through Christ is the most vital outcome of healing.

# Mark 8:34-38
## [Matthew 16:24-28; Luke 9:23-27]

Not the easiest passage to interpret. It might be for some that this passage means accepting one's illness or infirmity as one's cross and simply carrying it for the sake of Christ. A great deal of historic Christian asceticism [hardship] reads this passage in such a way. Some even deliberately allow hardship to come their way so that they might deliberately experience the sufferings of Christ. Some continental Catholic spirituality is in that tradition.

But the passage allows a further reading. For some people who have experienced God's hand in healing - perhaps through medical intervention, perhaps through requested or spontaneous prayer, perhaps through both - there is perhaps a harder cross to carry. Many other passages speak of Jesus' miracles being accompanied by an instruction from him to the healed person for the person to witness, to be an evangelist, to be a missionary spreading his word.

Many if not all will readily accept God's healing. But many find it harder to accept the command to give thanks to God by engaging in evangelism. This is a real cross for many.

Having gained the 'whole world' through bodily healing all is then lost and the challenge for witness and mission is missed.

The passage reminds us that following the way of Christ is also to enter into the ridicule and suffering he was to endure.

# Acts 19:10-12

There is a curious fascination with relics and items which are deemed to have healing properties because they have been associated with particularly holy people. We heard in an earlier bible study of the shadow of Peter and how people sought to be in it as Peter passed by. Here we have items of Paul's workwear - the handkerchief and the apron of the tanner or tent maker being employed as relics - seemingly with healing properties.

Whether it is the items themselves that convey or enable the healing, or whether it is the simple, trusting faith of those who seek it. Or whether it is Our Lord who can work his healing through any item of matter, whether a lump such as me or a scrap of a holy man's clothing is it seems to me, entirely beside the point. If the outcome is the same and one can give glory to God as the result little else matters. What must be guarded against however, is veneration of the person or the material. They were simply the channels of God's grace. Ultimately all things come from him, and of his own must we return to him - this includes the blessings of his healing.

# Acts 19:13-17

There are problems in the interpretation of this set of verses. However the story is likely to be a true narrative for other manuscripts speak about exorcists of ancient days who would use the name of Jesus to ply their trade. Quite who Sceva was were are not sure, and whether he had seven sons we are not sure. But what seems likely is that those who were carrying out these exorcisms were likely to be maintaining their duty to the cult of Roman Emperor worship. Using the name of Jesus was therefore a blasphemy for it was employing his name for less than worthy ends.

Malevolent though they were the evil spirits who were the subject of the exorcisms would recognise and take advantage of this falsehood.

There is a warning in this passage that exorcisms should be rigorously and carefully controlled; by no means a ministry to take lightly nor yet to enter in any way that is unsupervised.

It could be said that verses 18-20 give the story a good ending! That is unlikely for many of the passages cited above record confession of faith, or the injunction to evangelistic activity arising from a healing.

We need not therefore be surprised to find many believers who took the opportunity to rid themselves of their occult libraries - libraries of which they were perhaps ashamed to confess they had previously amassed. Through their action the power of God was portrayed.

# James 5:14-16

Broadly speaking Peter dominates Act 2 - 11 with his teaching and preaching. From Acts 12 onwards it is Paul - with his missionary journeys outwards from Jerusalem and James - with his focus on the centre of the early Church, Jerusalem. James' centrality in Jerusalem is the natural complement to Paul's missionary travel away from it, though we must never forget Paul always referred back to Jerusalem at and as the centre.

In the Eastern Orthodox Church the centrality of James in the corpus of Biblical texts is given by his letter being placed immediately after the Acts of the Apostles. James' concern therefore to balance the life of faith as one of action and prayer comes as the natural sequel to Paul's missionary travels as recorded in Acts. James' concern that the people engage in pastoral work, given in these verses, is therefore seen with the importance it deserves and which the church has given it since earliest times.

# Hebrews 5:7-10

A great deal of Christian spirituality and devotional writing as well as practice has revolved around the merits of suffering as a virtue to be sought and even on occasion deliberately induced.

In Poland and Portugal there are pilgrimage routes which the faithful are expected to follow on their knees - rejoicing as they do that the pain reminds them of the wounds of Christ. Nearer home the hairshirt tradition of the ascetics of the Middle Ages seems a long way away from us today - the enforced rigorism and almost ritualised suffering too morbidly attached to a notion of a suffering Christ who I believe is *not* found in the Scriptures.

The writer of the letter to the Hebrews refers to Jesus' agony in the garden when he writes, 'he offered prayers and supplications ... to him who was able to save him from death'.

The word 'offered' is an allusion to the temple's sacrificial cultus. It implies here that Christ's agony of prayer in the garden of Gethsemane was a representative act, summing up and representing before God all the entreaties of people in their hour of need.

The addition of the phrase prayers and supplications were common combinations. The former emphasising the need which brings about the action, the latter being suggestive of the manner of the prayer of the desparate person approaching an innevitable end of life.

The fact that Jesus prayed for himself displays his total humanity. I sometimes hear people saying, 'I know I shouldn't pray for myself' - why on earth not, Jesus prayed for himself. Why shouldn't you - so long as your prayers for yourself complement those for others.

We know from the Gospels something of the content of the prayer in Gethsemane. 'Take this cup from me'. Knowing God could save him from death Jesus prayed to him for this. His prayer was made to 'him who was able to save him from death'.

Don't be tempted to put sugar on the bitterness of this sentence to sweeten the interpretation. Jesus did not say he wanted to be delivered safely through death into a new life. He wanted to escape the fact of death and the suffering which would in all probability accompany it.

As we and as the writer to the Hebrews knew, the petition was not granted. But prayed in complete submission to the will of God Jesus knew his prayer had been heard by God. The result was that he 'was set free from fear'. By this I mean that Jesus, through his prayer being heeded rather than granted, 'was set free from fear'. It is noticeable how, in the Gospels, after the agony in the garden Jesus goes forward to meet his captors and then the summary trial before his execution with a calm dignity.

Through his prayers his fear of death was removed. There seems some connection between the obedience shown by Jesus and the suffering he underwent. Although he was Son of God, he learned obedience to God from what he suffered at human hands.

He learnt that prayer can meet with an answer very different from that which is requested. He learnt too, to submit himself to the very conditions from which he had asked to be freed.

It is only in the privileged North and West of the globe where freedom from suffering can be taken for granted by the majority of us. It is the minority who are ill who remind us that suffering is around the corner all the time. For most other people around the world, suffering is part and parcel of being human. For us we seek to avoid it. Yet in suffering we find an occasion [dare I call it an opportunity?] to go the way of Christ and enter into both the actuality and the reality of his life of obedience and his freedom from fear.

But to do this we must enter into the depths of his anxiety about his approaching death and through confidence that our prayer is being heard by God be obedient to the way he is leading us.

From this reading it is clear that Jesus did not seek his suffering - in the manner of the mediaeval monk let's say, or the Polish Pilgrim, but rather had to - was forced to confront the innevitable reality of the suffering he could not avoid.

One of my best friends from college days is the prior of a small monastery of hermit monks. They live a very ascetical life, but without enforced hardship. The life revolves around prayer, living according to need, study, talk and work as is necessary to make living possible and without distraction.

Although monastic, there is something here for us. Do not seek out suffering to enhance your prayer life or to make you closer to Christ. Christ himself didn't and doesn't want you to.

Live obediently and carefully, seeking to avoid suffering, but where it has to be faced, do so obediently and with confidence in the path Christ is laying out before you.[4]

# 2 Kings 4:25b-37

The background is that a child had been promised to a woman as a response to her kindness to Elisha and his servant Gehazi. The son was born, was growing up, but when out in the fields was taken seriously ill with head pains and we are told, died very quickly. The mother set out immediately to seek out Elisha.

Her address to him is both begging and pleading. Why had Elisha promised her a child when sorrow of such magnitude was to befall her. Without hesitation Elisha had given his instructions to Gehazi who carried them out. The boy showed no signs of recovery. Elisha then himself sought to effect the boy's recovery which he did by means of repeated bodily warming. In prostration before Elisha the woman gave thanks.

I want to note the place Gehazi had in this tale. The two following studies will focus upon this.

# 2 Kings 5:1-19a

Naaman, a mighty warrior was also a leper. His first, mistaken, approach for healing was to the king of Israel. His second was to Elisha but upon hearing the command to wash and be clean was angry. Naaman seemed to demand a much more dramatic event than is evidenced by simple washing. His servants petitioned him and he obeyed the command to wash.

Upon his cleansing he affirmed faith in the God of Elisha and offered payment; payment which Elisha refused. All he asked subsequently was pardon for worshipping in a pagan temple when his master required him to go with him to help him physically.

Gehazi obviously heard the interchange but was silent.

# 2 Kings 5:19b-27

Gehazi now comes to the centre-stage. Unhappy that no payment had been extracted from Naaman he rode after Naaman and extracted payment by deception. Elisha aware of this rebuked Gehazi for his deception. Gehazi, unlike the woman of 2 Kings 4 and Naaman had not we are told seen fit to give thanks for the healing. Wanting earthly reward he had lied to get it. Punishment was due him. He took Naaman's leprosy.

Healing involves giving thanks to God, shunning sin and turning to live a new life seeking no reward but every opportunity to give him the praise for the wonders he does.

# 1 Kings 17:17-24

The context of this passage is given in the verses which precede it. Elijah had been given hospitality at the house of the widow of Zarephath. Although without food she had offered the water she had; in return for this generosity Elijah gave his word that she should never lack. However in this passage her son dies and the woman, angry that the prophet's presence had caused her sins to be revealed berates him for darkening her door.

Elijah, sharing the anguish of the woman, reviles God for his apparent lack of care for the woman and her son. Without waiting for answer he proceeds to take actions which, it would seem, would seek to bring about the son's restoration to life. Then, we are told, God heard Elijah's angry call to him, and listening to it, the 'breath of life returned to the boy'.

The woman recognised Elijah's authority to come from God.

Whether the story is to be treated literally or as a metaphor of the life-giving force of the word of God breathed into people we cannot say. Either way, the woman was no longer to be bound to her past sin, nor yet to view Elijah's presence as God's way of reminding her of it; nor was she to view her son's death as God's punishment.

# CHAPTER NOTES

## Introduction
1   Further reading around this area can be found in Morris Maddocks, *The Christian Healing Ministry* pp.153-157.

## Unit 1
1   Ian T. Ramsey, *Religious Language*, SCM London 1974, p.24.

## Unit 3
1   Maddocks, *The Christian Healing Ministry* p.17. A great deal of material in this chapter has been drawn from Maddocks.
2   Thomas 113.

## Unit 4
1   Maddocks, *The Christian Healing Ministry* p.56.
2   *Apostolic Constitutions, VIII:1* in Alexander Roberts and James Donaldson (ed.), *Anti-Nicene Christian Library vol. XVII.*
3   Roger Vaughan, *Saints for Healing,* Leader's Manual pp.50-51.

## Unit 5
1   Roger Vaughan, *Saints for Healing,* Leader's Manual p.20.

## Unit 6
1   Maddocks, *The Christian Healing Ministry* pp.60-61.
2   Michael Ramsey, *The Christian Priest Today*, SPCK 1973 and re-printed many times since. This book has an excellent chapter entitled 'The Priest as Absolver'.
3   Churches should keep three oils. One for use in baptism, one for healing and the third [Chrism] is a balm of oil and spices [eg frankin-cense and myrrh] for use at confirmation and ordination.

## Unit 7
1   *A Memorandum on Exorcism*, The Church in Wales 1974.
2   Maddocks, *The Christian Healing Ministry* pp.128-129.
3   See the Bible studies on deliverance.

4    *Church Times*, 4th April 1975.
5    Mary Pytches, *A Healing Fellowship*, p.133.
6    Mary Pytches, *op. cit.* p.131.
7    David Pytches, *Come, Holy Spirit*, pp.211-212.
8    Stuart Hall, *Doctrine and Practice in the Early Church*, p.18.
9    *Ibid.*
10    Hippolytus, *Apostolic Constitution:* 21,22, quoted from *A New Eusebius,* ed. J.Stevenson, SPCK 1970.
11    Quoted from my own doctoral dissertation, *Person and Experience: a Study in the Thought of Edgar Sheffield Brightman* [unpublished], University of St Andrews 1991, p.8.
12    Letter of November 23rd 1993.

## Bible Studies on Healing

1    John Richards, *But Deliver us from Evil: an Introduction to the demonic dimension in pastoral care*, Darton, Longman and Todd 1988, London 1988, p.13.
2    C.S.C. Williams, *The Acts of the Apostles*, A. & C. Black, London 1985 p.275.
3    Morna D. Hooker, *A Commentary on the Gospel According to Mark*, A. & C. Black 1991 p.147.
4    From a sermon of my own at St Andrew's Episcopal Church, St Andrews, Lent 5 1994, drawing on exegesis by Hugh Montefiore in his *Commentary on Hebrews*, A. & C. Black 1987.

# GENERAL BIBLIOGRAPHY

*A Memorandum on Exorcism*, The Church in Wales, 1974

*A New Eusebius*, ed. J. Stevenson, SPCK, 1970

Angela Ashwin, *Heaven in Ordinary*, Mayhew and McCrimmon.

Rita Bennett, *How to Pray for Inner Healing*, Kingsway

Reginald East, *Heal the Sick*, Hodder and Stoughton.

Jim Cotter, *Healing - More or Less*, Cairns Publications, 1990

Jane Grayshorn, *A Pathway Through Pain*, Kingsway.

John Gunstone, *The Lord is our Healer*, Hodder and Stoughton.

John Gunstone, *Baptised in the Spirit?*, Highland Books.

Stuart Hall, *Doctrine and Practice in the Early Church*, SPCK, 1991

Hippolytus, *Apostolic Constitution*: 21,22, quoted from *A New Eusebius*, ed. J.Stevenson, SPCK, 1970

Joyce Huggett, *Listening to God* and *Listening to Others*, Hodder and Stoughton.

Gerard W. Hughes, *Oh God, Why?*, Bible Reading Fellowship, 1993.

Basil Hume OSB, *To be a Pilgrim - A spiritual notebook*, SPCK.

Andrew Knock, *The Purpose of Your Church*, General Synod of the Scottish Episcopal Church, 1989.

Peter Kreeft, *Making Sense out of Suffering*, Hodder and Stoughton

R.A. Lambourne, *Community, Church and Healing*, Arthur James, London, 1987

C.S. Lewis, *A Grief Observed* and *The Problem of Pain*, Fontana

Francis MacNutt, *The Power to Heal*, Ave Maria Press

Francis MacNutt, *Healing*, Hodder and Stoughton

Morris Maddocks, *The Christian Healing Ministry*, SPCK 1990

Morris Maddocks, *Twenty Questions About Healing*, SPCK

Michael Mitton, *The Wisdom to Listen*, Grove Pastoral Series 5

David Pytches, *Come Holy Spirit*, Hodder and Stoughton

Mary Pytches, *Set My People Free*, Hodder and Stoughton

Ian T. Ramsey, *Religious Language*, SCM, London 1974

John Richards, *But deliver us from evil: An Introduction to the demonic dimension in pastoral care*, DLT 1974

John Richards, *The Question of Healing Services*, Daybreak

ed. John Richards, *The Church's Healing Ministry*, Marshall Pickering

David Runcorn, *Space for God*, Daybreak

David Seamands, *Healing of Memories*, Scripture Press

Ruth Carter Stapleton, *The Gift of Inner Healing*, Hodder and Stoughton

Leo Thomas and Jan Alkire, *Healing As A Parish Ministry: Mending Body, Mind and Spirit*, Ave Maria Press, Notre Dame, Indiana 1992

Roger Vaughan, *Saints for Healing*, Anglican Renewal Ministries, Derby, 1991 [reprint]

C.S.C. Williams, *The Acts of the Apostles*, A. & C. Black, London 1985

John Wimber, *Power Healing*, Hodder and Stoughton

John Wimber, *Power Evangelism*, Hodder and Stoughton


# OTHER RESOURCES:

**The Acorn Healing Trust,**
The Rt. Revd. Morris Maddocks,
Whitehill Chase, High Street, Bordon, Hampshire GU35 0AP

**Anglican Renewal Ministries,**
45 Friar Gate, Derby DE1 1DA
[see in particular the title, *Saints for Healing*, in the GENERAL BIBLIOGRAPHY. This little work gave a great deal of insight in the preparation of *A WAY FOR HEALING*.

**The Christian Fellowship of Healing,**
The Eric Liddell Centre,
Holy Corner, Morningside Road, Edinburgh EH10

# A PRAYER FOR HEALING

Loving Father, we praise your name
that you have drawn close to us in Christ Jesus
and given your healing gift
in the power of your Holy Spirit.

Thank you for your promise
that through the healing you offer,
the sick will find health.


Father, forgive us when do not pray as we ought
and forgive us all we do
which would stop us coming closer to you.

Father God, we accept your healing for our need -
- humbly, gratefully and completely.
We thank you for it and give You the glory.


Show us what to do to put faith into love
so that you may be glorified,
your Word obeyed,
and your Holy Spirit heard.

Amen.

# APPENDIX

A Review of *A Way for Healing* by Richard Bauckham, Professor of New Testament Studies at The University of St. Andrews

The best reviewer for this book would really be someone who has used it in a study group, as it is intended to be used. I have not done that, and I did not attempt all the exercises. But I did find myself constantly stimulated to the kinds of thought that should have been part of a group discussion. Not surprisingly, the more theological parts had this effect on me, but also especially thought-provoking are the many stories quoted in the book, not just as illustrations but often as ways of posing issues and inviting discussion. I was glad to find I could not always tell whether my conclusion was the 'right' one. All this bodes well for its use as a workbook.

There is an admirable blend of serious theology, clearly explained, and sensitive engagement with practical reality. This is a field in which theory that is not grounded in experience and tested by experience can be not only silly but also dangerous. Bob Gillies is aware of this and treads carefully.

In three areas I would have liked to find more discussion. First, I would have valued a fuller account of healing as a total process involving a variety of elements - medicine, prayer, psychological factors, social support, and so on - and of God's power as working through all of these. Such an account would head off the dangers of isolating the 'spiritual' dimension as uniquely the channel through which God works and of seeing any competition or contradiction between say, medicine and prayer. Healing is always a complex process which no one fully understands, and so there is no need to make sharp distinctions between 'miraculous' healings and healings which medicine alone effects.

Secondly to talk about healing we need some idea of what a state of health or wholeness would be. Otherwise we do not know what needs healing. But these things are not self-evident. We all know disabled people who live much fuller lives than many people with no disability. We all know the good that has come out of living and struggling with problems we thought too much for us and would have preferred removed. But we live in a society obsessed with health and fitness, and a society which encourages people to think every problem must have a solution. We must be very careful not to confuse God's desire for wholeness with whatever sort of physical or emotional well-being people are influenced by our culture to want.

Finally, a Christian concern with healing must go further than the individual: to the healing of our sick society and the healing of our badly damaged relationship with nature. And these are not just other things. We are only just realising how much physical ill-health is caused by pollution, and how much emotional ill-health and crime are the products of advanced industrial society with its distortion of human relationships and alienation from nature. Prayer for healing also needs to reach as far as these root causes of our problems, which are just as realistically demonic as individual experiences with the occult are. God's purpose is the healing of his whole creation.

Perhaps I am asking for a sequel! But meantime I look forward to the effects which the use of this workbook is surely going to have in St. Andrew's and elsewhere.*

* From *The Net*, the magazine of St Andrew's Episcopal Church, St Andrews, December 1993

# Other Books on the subject of HEALING from the Handsel Press

CHRISTIAN ETHICS IN HEALTH CARE  by John Wilkinson
A major text book by a doctor and theologian. £27.50.

ACROSS THE SPECTRUM  by Ian Cowie
A guide to the search for spiritual meaning today - covers dowsing, alternative medicine, witchcraft and much else. £7.95.

GOD's GREEN GIFTS  by Joe Leckie
A plea for proper study and use of renewable energy sources. £4.95.

*Available from your local bookshop or in case of difficulty from Carberry Tower, Musselburgh EH21 8PY (add £1 for handling and postage).*